Lanai Island Hawaii. USA

Travel and Tourism

Author
Caleb Gray.

SONITTEC PUBLISHING. All rights reserved. No part of this publication may be reproduced, distributed, or transmitted in any form or by any means, including photocopying, recording, or other electronic or mechanical methods, without the prior written permission of the publisher, except in the case of brief quotations embodied in critical reviews and certain other noncommercial uses permitted by copyright law. For permission requests, write to the publisher, addressed "Attention: Permissions Coordinator," at the address below.

Copyright © 2019 Sonittec Publishing
All Rights Reserved

First Printed: 2019.

`

Publisher:
SONITTEC LTD
College House, 2nd
Floor
17 King Edwards
Road,
Ruislip
London
HA4 7AE

Table of Content

SUMMARY 1
ABOUT LANAI 6
HISTORY OF LANAI 17
    BEFORE LANAI ISLAND WAS INHABITED 18
    THE FIRST INHABITANTS OF THE HAWAIIAN ISLANDS 19
    HUMAN CONTACT 21
    HOW LANAI WAS INHABITED 23
    THE ARRIVAL OF KING KAMEHAMEHA I 25
    THE 1900S TO THE PRESENT 26
THE CULTURAL SCENE IN LANAI 29
    THE PEOPLE OF LANAI 39
TOURISM 50
    LANAI CITY, LANAI 54
    THINGS TO SEE IN LANAI 62
    TOURIST ATTRACTIONS AND FESTIVALS IN LANAI 74
    CUISINE OF LANAI 85
    MANELE BAY, LANAI 96
        Manele Bay, Lanai on a Budget 105
        How to Get to Manele Bay, Lanai 113
        What to Do in Manele Bay, Lanai 117
        Where to Stay in Manele Bay, Lanai 126
    NEIGHBORHOODS 135
    SPORTING ACTIVITIES IN LANAI 145
    THE CUISINE OF LANAI 155
    WHAT TO DO IN LANAI 166
    GETTING TO LANAI 177
    TIPS AND TRICKS FOR THE TRAVELER 179

Lanai Island, Hawaii. USA

Summary

The importance of travelling in our life?
Everyone has their very own reasons to travel. Some people travel for work, some travel for pleasure while for others it is just a way of life. They travel to live and to escape at the same time.

Whatever might be the reason to travel, here are few ways in which travelling would definitely change you and I think that is why travelling becomes so important in life:

<u>Enjoy being alone</u>: There is something therapeutic about being alone and being at peace with it.

While you soak in a new culture, you also connect with your own inner self.

<u>Learn to adapt</u>: It is a different world out there, literally. Be it the pace of life, the language or simply the change in weather, it is always a change and you have to adapt to it. This is what makes travelling truly beautiful as you break away from the routine and adapt to something totally new.

<u>Experience a new culture</u>: Every place comes with its distinct cultural habits, you cannot think about New York without talking about its fast paced life and about Italy without enjoying its relaxed lifestyle. Similarly, while visiting the UK you might have to be a bit formal in your interactions with the locals, on the other hand, while greeting the people in Thailand, one can be really warm and casual.

Lanai Island, Hawaii. USA

<u>Broaden your taste buds</u>: Travelling without experiencing the local food is just not complete. It is not only a culinary experience but a cultural one as well.

<u>Get out of comfort zone</u>: From simple experiences like the weather, way of life or food to the more adventurous ones like trying a new sport, travelling really pushes ones boundaries to the core. You might end up participating in a street carnival in Brazil just like the locals or trying the local delicacies (read insects) in Thailand.

<u>Indulge in Photography</u>: It does not matter whether you are a professional or not. It is also irrelevant whether you have a DSLR or a very basic camera, while travelling what matters is the love and quest for seeing beautiful places and the sheer joy of capturing them in your lense. Travelling would in return give you your very own collection

of amazing postcards of beautiful sunsets, snow laced mountains or sunny beaches.

<u>Learn to escape</u>: Travelling is the best way to break the routine. If you are in a bustling city, go ahead and experience the country life. If you are in a rural place, travel to a bustling city and experience its madness. Stressed with the city life or work pressure? A spa break in Himalayas or Kerala is a must try.

<u>Appreciate Nature</u>: The quest to explore more when one is travelling always leads to a sense of amazement about nature. While most of us keep a track of technological advancements, Nature has its own ways of outshining all of these. The Antelope Canyon in Arizona or Turquoise Ice in Russia are the finest examples of this. For more, check out the most unbelievable places around the world.

Lanai Island, Hawaii. USA

<u>Get closer to your own roots</u>: While one travels and experiences a lot of different cultures and practices, it definitely brings one closer to his or her own roots. Travel helps one appreciate one's identity and culture.

Travelling is all about experiences. They can happen in terms of culture, people, places but most importantly with one's own self and this was all about

About Lanai

Lanai

The island of Lanai, located almost in the middle of the Hawaiian Islands, is a tourist treat just waiting to be explored by anyone who wants to experience Hawaii in a unique way. While some of the bigger islands of Hawaii are packed with grand tourist attractions, resplendent hotels, and loads of vacationers, the island of Lanai presents a more laid-back and intimate atmosphere. In a place with no stop lights and hardly any paved roads, it's easy to see why Lanai can be the perfect vacation destination. Whether you are planning a trip with a loved one or a bunch of friends, you should definitely consider visiting the island of Lanai. This article will give you some basic information about Lanai and what makes this island such a unique destination.

Geography and climate
As mentioned above, one of the unique things about Lanai is that there aren't too many people crowding this small island. As one of the smallest inhabited islands, Lanai has a population of just over 3,000 people, plus the number of tourists who visit the island year-round. Out of Hawaii's eight main islands, Lanai is the sixth largest at a little over 140 square miles, which is even smaller than cities like Los Angeles and New York. At its widest point, Lanai island is only 18 miles across, which means that you can practically explore the entire island, even if you only have a short vacation there. The island has about 47 miles of shoreline for you to explore and experience to the

fullest. Breathtaking vistas, beautiful beaches, as well as its intriguing history and culture make up for what Lanai lacks in size.

Aside from the size of the island, another unique feature of Lanai's geography is its dramatic topography. From the island's white sand beaches, the land elevates as you go further inland. The highest point on Lanai island is Lana'ihale, which is a rain forest that reaches an elevation of over 3,300 feet. If you are adventurous enough to take a trip up this volcanic mountain, you can get great views of Lanai, as well as other Hawaiian islands. The geography and topography of Lanai is a large part of what makes this island such a wonderful place to visit, from clear blue oceans and pure white beaches to lush green forests and lunar-like rock formations.

With such a diverse geography, you might expect that Lanai has an equally diverse climate. The truth is, the climate in Lanai is relatively cool. Island temperatures range from a little over 60 to 70 degrees Fahrenheit, with the hottest areas down by the beach and the coolest at the peak of Lana'ihale. You may want to bring a jacket or sweater to keep you warm if you decide to go up the mountain. If you are staying in Lanai City, which is at about 1700 feet, the temperature averages a little over 70 degrees Fahrenheit during the warmest months. While some of the islands of Hawaii get covered in loads of rainfall, the climate of Lanai is relatively dry, with an annual rainfall average of under 40 inches.

Privacy and peace
One of the most unique things about the island of Lanai is that it's one of the few main islands where you can still get some privacy and peace. Although

many of the other islands do have some quiet areas that you can retreat to, the entire island of Lanai can be seen as a quiet retreat where you don't need a "do not disturb" sign to get some privacy. Other inhabited Hawaiian islands, such as the Big Island, Maui, and Oahu, are packed not only with tourists but also with locals. Lanai is largely uninhabited and those who do live on Lanai are mainly concentrated in Lanai City.

What this means is that you won't have to go a long way just to get some peace and quiet.

Because Lanai is still largely uninhabited and not fully developed, it is often called "The Secluded Isle," a place where you can get away from the daily hassles of traffic jams, congested cities, and noise pollution. Most of the time, the only things you'll be hearing on the island are the occasional bird songs, the blowing wind, and the soft waves.

For this reason, Lanai is often advertised as a great place to go for honeymoons or romantic getaways.

Places to stay
One of the reasons Lanai is such a peaceful and private destination is because there are only a few places to stay on the island. Most of the other main islands of Hawaii are packed full of resorts, hotels, lodges, and other accommodation options. The most popular hotels on the island are the two luxurious resorts: Lodge at Koele and the Four Seasons Resort Lanai. The Lodge at Koele is located in Lanai City, which most people refer to as "the village." Meanwhile, the Four Seasons Resort Lanai is further south, at Manele Bay. Aside from these award-winning resorts, there are also a number of bed and breakfast accommodations around the island, or you can just camp out along the beaches or in the park.

A unique history

Another unique aspect of the island of Lanai is its unique history. Lanai was inhabited around 1,000 years after some of the other islands of Hawaii. The reason it took so long for the place to be inhabited is not only because it is a small, isolated island, but also because the Hawaiian legends believed that man-eating evil spirits occupied the island. The ancient Hawaiians only inhabited the islands after the son of a Maui chief was banished to the island. When the chief saw that his son's fire burned bright along the shores of Lanai, he had his son picked up and returned to Maui island. For his son's bravery, the Maui chief rewarded him with control over Lanai. The chief and his son encouraged immigrants to the island and, as the island was inhabited by more people, the ancient Hawaiians left their mark on the island, leaving behind petroglyphs, religious temples, and other historical landmarks.

In the late 1700s, Kamehameha I came to Lanai and practically killed everyone on the island in a war for control of Lanai. King Kamehameha I did not spare the island much mercy, going as far as burning practically all of the remains on the island after killing its inhabitants. Kamehameha I had a vision to unite all of the islands of Hawaii to create the Kingdom of Hawaii, and he succeeded. Although he wiped out the island, King Kamehameha I returned to the island numerous times, because he had a favorite fishing retreat there called Kaunolu, which you can still visit today.

Another unique aspect of Lanai's history is that the island was bought by James Dole in the 1920s. Dole and his company turned Lanai into one of the largest pineapple plantations in the entire world. Much of the island was converted into a pineapple plantation, which produced much of the world's pineapple supply. You can still visit the site of this massive pineapple plantation, although not much of it remains, with less than 100 acres of pineapples used for local consumption. As the pineapple and agriculture industry as a whole began to decline, the James Dole's company was reformed into Castle & Cooke, which was bought and owned by David H. Murdock in 1985. Castle & Cooke is largely responsible for shifting the development and economy of Lanai to tourism. Today, you can visit many of the historical sites in Lanai by 4-wheel drive vehicle or hiking.

Some unique sites to visit in Lanai
Munro Trail - This popular trail is just minutes north of Lanai City and stretches for about seven miles--climbing Lana'ihale mountain and snaking around Lanai City, before heading south toward Manele Bay. Here you can get beautiful views of the city, Maunalei gulch, and the neighboring

islands. You can explore this trail by 4x4 or by hiking.

The Garden of the Gods - Keahiakawelo is one of the most unique places in the Hawaiian Islands. This site is home to rock formations that can only be described as lunar-like. Because of the odd yet beautiful rock formations at Keahiakawelo, it is often referred to as the Garden of the Gods. Be sure not to miss out on this interesting natural wonder.

Hulopoe Bay - Ranked as one of the best beaches in the United States, Hulopoe Bay is a place where you can go to snorkel, have a picnic, relax on the beach, body board, swim, and see the Spinner dolphins. You may want to avoid this place during winter, though, because the water conditions can get a little rough.

Island culture

If you want to experience Hawaii for its raw natural beauty and laid-back island culture, then there is no better place for you to go to than the island of Lanai. In a place with no stop lights, no traffic jams, world-class resorts, and some of the world's most unique sights, Lanai island is like a paradise within a paradise

History of Lanai

Located southeast of Oahu, south of Molokai, and east of Maui, Lanai sits practically in the center of the Hawaiian archipelago. As one of the smallest inhabited islands, Lanai is a testament to the saying that "good things come in small packages." Whether you are going to Hawaii to stay on Lanai island or just plan on passing by while island-hopping, this wonderful island offers a variety of things to do and places to experience. The island of Lanai is often referred to as "The Pineapple Isle" or "The Secluded Isle." These two names give some insight into the history of this beautiful Hawaiian island. Read on to learn more about Lanai and its interesting history.

Before Lanai island was inhabited

Before going into the history of Lanai itself, it's important to look into how the Hawaiian Islands were formed and inhabited. Millions of years ago, long before man roamed the earth, the tectonic plates and volcanoes of the Pacific Ring were busy forming what we know today as the Hawaiian Islands. The Hawaiian Islands were formed by one of the largest geological hot spots in the world. A geological hot spot is basically a stationary reservoir that produces large amounts of magma. As the magma is pushed through the earth's surface and into the waters of the oceans, the magma cools and solidifies. The hot spots continue to produce magma, which is pushed upwards, forming underwater mountains that can break the surface of the water to create islands.

Although these hot spots are stationary, the earth's crust sits on moving tectonic plates that shift and rotate. The Hawaiian Islands are located on the Pacific Plate. As the Pacific Plate shifted and rotated, the stationary hot spot continued to push magma through the crust, eventually creating each of the islands of Hawaii. The first of the Hawaiian Islands to be created around six million years ago is Kauai. After Kauai came Oahu, Molokai, Lanai, Maui, the Big Island, and Loihi.

The first inhabitants of the Hawaiian Islands

The Hawaiian Islands were barren for quite a long time, because of the distance that separates the archipelago from the mainland. The first inhabitants of Lanai and the Hawaiian Islands, in general, were the plants. Because the Hawaiian Islands are thousands of miles from any mainland continent, nature played a huge role in getting the first plants and animals on the islands. The seeds of plants were carried to the islands by the winds and the sea currents. Birds also helped to bring some of the plant life to Hawaii as they flew over the islands while migrating around the globe.

Many of the first forms of animal life on the Hawaiian Islands were birds and forms of sea life that evolved to inhabit the lands. The isolated islands were too far from the mainland for reptiles and land mammals to travel to. The plants and animals that first inhabited the Hawaiian Islands had millions of years to evolve. Today, there are numerous species of plant and animal life that are unique to the Hawaiian Islands.

Human contact

The first people to come to Hawaii were the Polynesians from the Marquesas Islands. Arriving on the islands some time between 300 A.D. and 600 A.D., these people made their first settlements along the shores of Hawaii, where they had access to water and food sources. Water is important not only for drinking, but also for agriculture. The natives from the Marquesas Islands made the first farms on the Hawaiian Islands, as they brought with them many types of food to plant and grow. Aside from bringing over taro, sugar cane, and other types of plants, these settlers are also responsible for bringing the first land mammals to the Hawaiian Islands. These natives brought with them animals such as dogs, pigs, and chickens.

A second wave of Polynesian settlers came around circa 1000. These Polynesians were from Tahiti, and they arrived on double-hulled canoes, large enough to serve as symbols of their success as a society and culture. When the Tahitians came to the Hawaiian Islands, they oppressed and alienated the first settlers from the Marquesas Islands, whom the Tahitians called commoners. As a result, those from the Marquesas fled further inland and up to the mountains, while the Polynesians from Tahiti settled on the more farm-friendly lands.

The Polynesians played a large role in inhabiting the Hawaiian Islands, establishing its culture, and forming its history. The Tahitians later run trade routes between Tahiti and the Hawaiian Islands, helping them to strengthen their economy, increase their population, and ultimately improve their life in Hawaii. As the natives cultivated the lands, they inhabited many of the main islands of Hawaii, including Oahu, Maui, and the Big Island.

They set up a social hierarchy that consisted of chiefs and the masses. The Polynesians also played a large role in introducing the first forms of religion and law, called the Kapu system, which was a system based on taboos and forbidden acts.

How Lanai was inhabited

Even though the Polynesians inhabited many of the Hawaiian Islands, Lanai was not one of them. For a long time, the natives thought that evil spirits lived in Lanai. This legend of man-eating spirits kept the natives from venturing to and settling on the island of Lanai. In the 1500s, though, Lanai got its first inhabitant: a man named Kauluaau. Kauluaau was banished to the island by his father, who was a chief on the island of Maui. It is said that Kauluaau went against the Kapu system by uprooting every breadfruit tree that he could find on Maui, so he was sentenced to be banished to the "evil" island of Lanai.

Though the natives believed that Kauluaau would never survive on the island, they were wrong. Every night, the chief would see Kauluaau's fire burning bright along the shores of Lanai, proving that he could brave the island and survive, despite the evil spirits that inhabited Lanai. Recognizing Kauluaau's courage and perseverance, the Maui chief had his son brought back to Maui. As a reward, chief Kakaalaneo gave his son control over the island of Lanai. Kauluaau encouraged the people to immigrate from Maui, Molokai, and other Hawaiian Islands. Much like how the rest of Hawaii was inhabited by humans, the first settlers on Lanai set up fishing villages along the shore. It was not long before they started farming and planting taro on the island's volcanic soil.

Lanai Island, Hawaii. USA

The arrival of King Kamehameha I

For hundreds of years, the island of Lanai was under the rule of the Mo'i, or king, of Maui until Kamehameha I set out to unite the Hawaiian Islands under one ruler: himself. It was widely believed that Kamehameha was the legendary warrior who was prophesied to unite the islands of Hawaii. It was this prophecy and the help of the first foreigners who landed on the Hawaiian Islands that made Kamehameha I the first King of the Kingdom of Hawaii in 1810.

Though some of the natives submitted to Kamehameha I, because he fulfilled the prophecy of the warrior king, others refused to recognize his leadership. He then killed many of the people who opposed to his rule. When Kamehameha I was on his mission for total control of the Hawaiian islands, he used many of the weapons that he got from the Europeans who first came to the islands in the 1770s. The natives had little chance to defend themselves from such powerful weapons, such as canons and guns. These weapons were used to kill many of the inhabitants of Lanai. In fact, Kamehameha I killed so much of Lanai's population in the 1700s that some Europeans coming to Hawaii in the 1790s decided not to land their ships on Lanai for the lack of settlements and inhabitants.

The 1900s to the present

Under King Kamehameha I's rule, the island of Lanai was once again inhabited and slowly developed into the island that we know today. The next big change in the history of Lanai came in 1922, when a man named James Dole purchased the entire island for around $1.1 million. Dole was the president of the Hawaiian Pineapple Company, which was later renamed Dole Food Company. Much of the lands here were used for pineapple plantations. Dole's efforts turned the island of Lanai into one of the largest pineapple plantations in the entire world, hence, its nickname "The Pineapple Isle."

When the pineapple industry started to plateau in the 1980s, Lanai underwent another major change, one that was in line with the changes that were occurring on many of the other Hawaiian Islands. As agriculture declined in Hawaii, the Dole Food Company had to be reformed into a new company named Castle & Cooke. When Dole Food Company CEO, David H. Murdock, bought Castle & Cooke, he also gained control over the Lanai island. Shifting away from agriculture, Castle & Cooke began developing Lanai as a tourist destination.

Today, there are hotels on the island of Lanai, as well as golf courses. The island's beautiful geography attracts many tourists who are looking to celebrate romance, adventure, or just a little R&R. Lanai has definitely had a rough history, but it is currently on the rebound as tourism leads the island and its inhabitants into another phase of its history. There are tons of things to do on the island of Lanai, from snorkeling and basking on the beach to 4x4 adventuring and viewing the Garden of the Gods. When you visit Lanai, make sure to take some time to visit some of its historical sites, meet its friendly people, and explore its beautiful geography.

Lanai Island, Hawaii. USA

The Cultural Scene in Lanai

With only more than a thousand permanent residents, Lanai is a definitely a small island. Lanai cannot boast of skyscrapers or complex road structures but Lanai prides itself of its rich and diverse culture - a culture that was made unique by the island's colorful past.

Added to the abundance of natural resources on the island is its very rich tradition and history. The people, the language, the literature, the religion, the cuisine, and the history of Lanai are as colorful as the sunset, the ocean, and the fields and the rain forests on the island.

Community

Lanai, the so-called "Secluded Island," is actually home to people of diverse roots. People with Japanese, Filipino, Polynesian, Portuguese, Korean, Chinese, and Spanish ancestry make up Lanai's population. In spite of this though, the people of Lanai consider themselves pure-blooded Lanaians. The people of this island are known for their friendliness and hospitality. Visitors who come here are always greeted by the locals with the warmest of smiles. The aloha spirit, which is always present and evident in each welcome, never ceases to impress the many tourists that come to the area.

Time seems to have been frozen on this island. The island's utter lack of the kind of sophistication that is usually found in many big cities allows its people a calm, relaxed and laid back lifestyle. Once there, you would also be able to feel it and you could forget about time while you drink in the beauty of everything that surrounds you on the island.

Although the island has a city, the ambiance of the place is much more like that of a village. This is probably one of the reasons why Lanai holds a special charm for visitors. The rustic simplicity of the island is really charming. The presence of the grand Four Seasons Resort on the island only adds to the enchanting atmosphere of the place. The contrast between the rusticity of the place and the sophistication of the resort makes the island look like one of those enchanted places in fairy tales.

Language
The language of the people of Lanai is as diverse as everything else on the island. There are two official languages in this island, English and Hawaiian. English is the language usually used in education. For many Lanaians, the native Hawaiian remains to be the language of their hearts. From the 1830s to

the 1950s, there was a decrease in the number of people who used the native Hawaiian language. It was because the United States subjugated Hawaii and English took the place of the native Hawaiian language. But after some time, the Hawaiian language resurfaced through the people's effort to promote the language in the schools. Many of the residents also use the Hawaiian Pidgin. During the heyday of the sugar plantations in Hawaii, there was a need to develop a language for the people from different races that flocked to Hawaii. Out of this came the Hawaiian Pidgin. It is a local dialect that is a combination of English and Hawaiian. Until today, Pidgin is used by many residents not just in Lanai, but in all the other islands of Hawaii.

Religion

The first religion in this island came from the Polynesians who came here thousands of years ago. The ancient Hawaiian religion was basically, polytheistic in nature. The ancient people of Lanai believed in various deities. The earliest Hawaiians, had both male and female deities. Aside from being polytheistic, the religion is also animistic, because they believe that powerful spirits reside in non-living things. One of the powerful deities that the earliest settlers believe in is Pele, the goddess of the volcano. According to accounts, the early people believed that Pele is actually present in the flowing lava. The first monarch of Hawaii, Kamehameha, was a follower of the early Hawaiian religion. It is said that he punished people who broke the kapu or the prohibitions imposed by the religion.

Christian missionaries also came to the Hawaiian islands and introduced Christinanity. Later, the Chinese came to the island and brought along their own religion. Then came the Japanese with their Buddhist and Shinto beliefs. Because of the fusion of the different beliefs and traditions, the religion of the ancient Hawaiians lost its great influence. In spite of that though, the ancient Hawaiian religion could still be seen and its spirit continues to live on until this day through the many ceremonies that are still held on the islands. The famous Hula dance itself is a religious practice that originated from this ancient Hawaiian religion. Today, this dance is performed during state ceremonies, festivals, and welcome parties.

Literature
The literature of the ancient people of Lanai, like in the rest of the islands of Hawaii, is oral in nature and is deeply rooted in religion. The "mele" (poetic language) is a chant through which the ancient people told their stories and honored their deities and chiefs. Today, the word "mele" is also used to mean "song."

One of the most important oral literature of the ancient settlers in this island is the Kumulipo, an epic poem and a chant, which is said to have been composed to honor a high chief.

The mele can be categorized into two, mele hula and mele oli. The former is a chant accompanied by musical instruments and a dance and is usually performed by several people. The latter, on the other hand, is a chant unaccompanied by musical instruments and is usually performed by just one person. In this type of hula, the focus is on the chant rather than on the dance.

Today, chanting is still performed during the Hula. During official state functions, for instance, Hula is performed as a form of prayer. It is usually accompanied by mele.

Myths and legends also abound in Lanai. One of the island's popular legends is that of Puu Pehe.

The story is said to have taken place in the offshore Sweetheart Rock located left of Hulopoe Bay. The legend tells about the maiden Puu Pehe who was kept in a cave near the rock by her lover. She drowned after a big wave washed the shore. With the help of the gods, her sweetheart buried her body on top of the rock before he himself leapt into the sea.

The people of Lanai explain through their legends the amazing geological features surrounding them. The existence of the awe-inspiring Keahiakawelo, for instance, has various mythical explanations. According to one account, the gods were so fond of creating art that they sent a strong wind to sculpt the rocks and boulders. Another explanation tells that the formations were created in order to house the spirits of the dead Hawaiian warriors. Still, a third version points to the the gods who dropped these rocks and boulders from the sky as they tended their garden.

Traditions

The spirit of aloha characterizes the tradition of the people. The Hula, for instance, is still performed to greet visitors. Aside from this, the luau, or the traditional Hawaiian party, is still held on this island. There is actually a resort in Lanai where you can request for a luau.

Cuisine

The staple food of the people of Lanai is still the traditional poi. But Lanaian cuisine is also influenced by various cultures that came in contact with the culture of the native Lanaians. Because of the abundance of marine life in the place, seafoods have always been a part of the cuisines of the people of Lanai. Today, many restaurants in the place also boasts of their seafood offerings. Expect therefore that Lanaian cuisine, seafood or not, will taste of many influences.

How Lanaian culture came to be so rich
The diverese culture of Lanai is the result of the various migrations of people to this island. The most important event that influenced the history of Lanai is when James Dole purchased the island and turned it into a pineapple plantation. Because the industry fared well, many people from China, Philippines, Japan, Hongkong, to name a few, were invited and were lured to go to Lanai to work in the plantation. This is why the culture of the people of Lanai, just like in the rest of Hawaii, is a hodgepodge of various cultural influences. You can see this intermingling of many different cultures in Lanai's traditions, language, religion, cuisine and in many other aspects of their lives. But it is well to remember that foreign influences did not start until the 1920s and that Lanai and the rest of

Hawaii had its own culture and traditions long before.

So if you want to visit a place teeming with diversity, not just in terms of environment, but also in terms of culture and tradition, Lanai should be on your list. On this island, you would not want for beautiful sights to see and you would be amazed at how so many diverse cultures could come together and form one very rich, unique and interesting culture.

The People of Lanai

Part of its small island charm is the unspoiled nature that makes it a tropical paradise. Lanai is painted with greenery because of its verdant rainforests and long stretch of grasslands. The setting sun also adds to the color of its surroundings, as it slowly fades into an orange sky, casting its shadow on the blue-sky ocean. The scenery, however, is not the only thing that's brightly painted. Lanai also has a colorful history, which makes this island worthy to be explored and discovered. The colorful history of the people of Hawaii is reflected through arts and its tradition, as seen on its lei, quilt, and the Hula.

History

The first settlers in Lanai were the Marquesas. They were Polynesians who came to the island more than a thousand years ago. Later, the Tahitians came to live in this island. During that time, Lanai was still regarded as an evil land, a place where sorcerers reside. Visiting Lanai back then was "kapu" or forbidden. In order to drive away the evil spirit, Prince Kaulalaau, a son of a Maui chief, exorcised the island. But this is just one of the legends about the Lanai Island. Some said that the prince was banished to the island and actually surprised many when glowing fire were seen from Maui. The Maui chief recognized his son's courage and let him take control of the island. The prince then encouraged people from other islands to inhabit the isolated Lanai.

According to some accounts, it was only in the 15th century that people started to come in waves to inhabit this island. In 1790, Lanai became part of the Kingdom of Hawaii after Kamehameha the Great unified the islands. At first, some of the native inhabitants opposed the great king's reign over the land, which led to mass killings. With no match to his weapons and power, eventually, they submitted to his rule.

Traders, whalers, and missionaries came to this island and cast their indelible influences in the culture and tradition of the people of Lanai. The course of Lanai history took a major turn when James Dole arrived in the island in 1922 and started his pineapple plantation. Because of the labor force required to run the plantation, jobs are plentiful in the island. People from various locations around the world migrated to Lanai to work in the pineapple plantation. Koreans, the Japanese, Chinese, Filipinos, and Portuguese are some of the early immigrants of this island. Producing a large part of the world's pineapple supply, it earned the nickname "The Pineapple Island."

Like the rest of the islands of Hawaii, Lanai is a melting pot of various cultures. The culture of the contemporary Lanaians can't be traced back to one specific group of people, because Hawaiian culture is actually a hodgepodge of cultural influences. The people of Lanai takes pride in this. In fact, the locals celebrate cultural diversity through its many festivals and events. One of the famous festivals in Lanai is the Festival of Aloha. This event is held usually in September to showcase the traditional dance in Hawaii, its music and history.

Traditions
The rich culture and tradition of the people of Lanai are reflected through their contemporary way of living. The sea food dishes that people in this island used to prepare are still present in local home tables and restaurants. Poi from taro is still considered a staple food of people in this island. The Kalua pig is also one of the popular dishes served during special occasions. Aside from its local cuisines, the island also takes pride in its dances and songs that came from the ancient settlers. The Lanaians of today, like the thousands of people who came before them, still perform the Hula and play the ukulele to greet visitors or to make the celebrations a great deal merrier.

Lanai is also home to folklore. The history of the island itself is deeply rooted to the myths and legends concocted by the early settlers. Lanai was once known as the "island of the ghost," inhabited by man-eating spirits and fiendish ghouls that are controlled by the sorceress Pahulu. It was said the the spirits were exorcised by Kaululaau, which encouraged people from other islands to inhabit the then secluded Lanai. Many people, even today, believe that there are still spirits roaming around the island. Some believe in the stories of the old about the Night Marchers who roam at night beating their drums, trying to find the entrance to the other world, or going to a battle to avenge their untimely death.

The stunning features of the island were also the setting of interesting legends. The beautiful rock formation Pu'u Pehe (the Sweetheart Rock) is said to be the place where the body of a young girl from Maui (Pu'u Pehe), who died of drowning, is buried by her lover. According to some, this 80-ft. rock is haunted by ghosts.

A vacation to Lanai won't be complete if you miss the amazing Keahikawelo, also known as the Garden of the Gods. This garden is not of lush greenery and blooming flowers. Instead, what you will see here are boulders and rocks of different shapes, sizes, and colors. Science explains the amazing rock formation as a result of the thousands years of erosion. However, the ancient people of Hawaii have their own stories to tell about the existence of this unique geological feature. The fascinating legends reflect the ingenuity of the ancient Lanaians in making up stories to explain the peculiarities of the things around them. One legend, for instance, tells that the rocks were formed to serve as a vessel that would house the spirits of the Hawaiian warriors. Another legend says that the boulders were accidentally dropped from the sky when gods tended their garden. Another story claims that these rocks and boulders are sculptures made by the gods who enjoyed artworks. In order to sculpt the rocks, the gods created strong winds.

The people of Lanai today
There are more than 3,000 people who consider Lanai their home. In this island, there is no such thing as ethnic majority, because everyone is part of a minority. Many Lanaians even claim that they have "mixed ethnicity." English and Hawaiian are the languages commonly used by people here; English is the spoken language, but Hawaiian remains the language of the heart for some. There are several people who use the Hawaiian Pidgin, a combination of English, Hawaiian, and other languages. In the past, the residents of Lanai earned their living by working in the pineapple plantation, but after the plantation closed down

and tourism opened, many residents are now working in hotels, restaurants, and other tourism-related workplaces.

The people of Lanai are best known for being laid-back. They are also among the world's friendliest people, always ready with their warm smiles to show their courtesy and generosity to visitors. Like their surroundings, their warmth and generosity are bountiful.

Those who call Lanai their home deeply appreciates nature's gift of beauty to their land. The Lanaians make efforts to protect their old fishing villages and the amazing topographical features of the place such as the Keahikawelo and the numerous beaches. Compared to other Hawaiian islands, Lanai is less developed. Not all areas are densely inhabited. In fact, there's no stop lights and barely any paved road. People here embrace simple ways of living and are very accommodating to guests who visit their island.

Although the island is relatively small, it has so much to offer in terms of natural wonders and activities. For city dwellers and impassioned travelers, the small island is a tropical paradise to rediscover. This is probably why its residents can't leave the island and tourists come to Lanai all-year round. The beaches in the island are not just ideal for swimming, they are also good spots for snorkeling, kayaking, and other thrilling water activities. One of the popular beaches here is the Hulopoe Beach. It is a wide stretch of sand surrounded by the azure water of the Pacific. Here, you will also get the chance to catch a glimpse of Spinner dolphins. With world-famous beaches, you can expect people here to be fun-loving and athletic. Often you'll see them lounging by the beach with sands between their toes and basking in the warmth of the sun or seaside breeze. Many of them are also into water sports such as surfing, swimming, diving, and kayaking.

There are so many things to do in Lanai, uncovering the rich history of the place, listening to the tales explaining how the wonderful structures came into being, experiencing the warmth of Lanaian welcome, and basking in the beauty and calmness that the place brings to everyone. The seclusion of the place and the rustic simplicity of the people's lifestyle also make the island an ideal place if you want to escape the bustling city life. The natural beauty and the serenity of the place will surely keep you at peace and reinvigorate your spirit.

Tourism

Lanai is not an easy place to reach. There are no direct flights from the mainland. It's almost as if this quiet, gentle oasis known, paradoxically, for both its small-town feel and its celebrity appeal demands that its visitors go to great lengths to get here in order to ensure that they will appreciate it.

Lanai (pronounced "Lah-*nigh*-ee"), the nation's biggest defunct pineapple patch, now claims to be one of the world's top tropical destinations. It's a bold claim because so little is here; Lanai has even fewer dining and accommodations choices than Molokai. There are no stoplights and barely 30 miles of paved road. This almost-virgin island is unspoiled by what passes for progress, except for a tiny 1920s-era plantation village and, of course, the village's fancy new arrivals: two first-class luxury hotels where room rates average $400-plus a night.

As soon as you arrive on Lanai, you'll feel the small-town coziness. People wave to every car, residents stop to "talk story" with their friends, fishing and working in the garden are considered priorities in life, and leaving the keys in your car's ignition is standard practice.

For generations, Lanai was little more than a small village, owned and operated by the pineapple company, surrounded by acres of pineapple fields. The few visitors to the island were either relatives of the residents or occasional weekend hunters. Life in the 1960s was pretty much the same as in the 1930s. But all that changed in 1990, when the

Lodge at Koele, a 102-room hotel resembling an opulent English Tudor mansion, opened its doors, followed a year later by the 250-room Manele Bay, a Mediterranean-style luxury resort overlooking Hulopoe Bay. Overnight the isolated island was transformed: Corporate jets streamed into tiny Lanai Airport, former plantation workers were retrained in the art of serving gourmet meals, and the population of 2,500 swelled with transient visitors and outsiders coming to work in the island's new hospitality industry. Microsoft billionaire Bill Gates chose the island for his lavish wedding, booking all of its hotel rooms to fend off the press and uncomplicated Lanai went on the map as a vacation spot for the rich and powerful.

But this island is also a place where people come looking for beauty, quiet, solitude, and an experience with nature. The sojourners who find their way to Lanai seek out the dramatic views, the tropical fusion of stars at night, and the chance to be alone with the elements.

They also come for the wealth of activities: snorkeling and swimming in the marine preserve known as Hulopoe Bay, hiking on 100 miles of remote trails, talking story with the friendly locals, and beachcombing and whale-watching along stretches of otherwise deserted sand. For the adventurous, there's horseback riding in the forest, scuba diving in caves, playing golf on courses with stunning ocean views, or renting a four-wheel-drive vehicle for the day and discovering wild plains where spotted deer run free.

In a single decade, a plain red-dirt pineapple patch has become one of Hawaii's top fantasy destinations. But the real Lanai is a multifaceted place that's so much more than a luxury resort and it's the traveler who comes to discover the island's natural wonders, local lifestyle, and other inherent joys who's bound to have the most genuine island experience.

Lanai City, Lanai

If you want to relax for awhile, gear away from the hustle and bustle of the city and book a vacation trip to Lanai. Lanai is a very small island in Maui County, Hawaii, which arose from a single volcanic mountain called "Lanai Hale." Lanai abounds in exquisite attractions and beautiful places to explore, especially Hawaii's famous historic district which can be found going downtown. It has a very small population that Lanai City itself became the island's main commerce and business area, where you can see several islands shops and restaurants to visit. Simply go downtown to the town square surrounding Dole Park. Here are some of the popular places you can visit to make your vacation in Lanai a very exciting and memorable one.

Koloiki Ridge

Koloiki Ridge is a sure favorite not only among the locals of Lanai, but also among various hikers and explorers visiting this beautiful island. You will tremendously enjoy the three-hour hiking in the wilds of the unpopulated Lanai, reaching up to the summit. The hike starts at the back of The Lodge at Koele, which is a favorite spot in Lanai, and there are also daily hikes starting from 11:00 am to 1:30 pm, offered at Koele, which amounts to $15 per person. You will be extremely delighted and awed to witness abounding greens and pine trees, not to mention the breathtaking glimpse of the romantic spot, Maunalei Valley, which is truly proven to be rich in both legend and natural beauty, making it a popular love spot for romantic couples. And what could be better after an exhausting but enjoyable hike than a peaceful retreat with nearby lodging. However, it is best that you choose lodging inside the town for more flexibility.

Shipwreck Beach

Shipwreck Beach is another equally astonishing place to visit while in Lanai, what with its untamed and stunning beauty that makes it a favorite stop-spot among many visitors to Lanai city. It offers an 8-mile stretch of sand ideal for sunbathing, picnicking, fishing, exploring, or simply walking. Shipwreck Beach is also the best body boarding and body-toning beach during summer. And since it is known for its very strong currents, it is not advised for swimming activities; although, beachcombers delight themselves with picking up brilliant shells and other treasures that are washed up on shore, making these sea gems unique mementos of Lanai on their way home.

Located along the northeastern coastline of Lanai, this beach can be reached only by a 4WD vehicle. From Lanai City, take Highway 44 to the end of the road, and then turn left on the dirt road to the parking area near the lighthouse ruins, with Shipwreck beach fronting the ruins, laying stretched in sand, for miles.

Polihua Beach

If you want to see a 1.5 miles long beach, go to the far northwestern tip of Lanai where you will see Polihua Beach, one of the longest white sand beaches usually visited by high winds and rough waters. That is why this beach is treated more of as a scenic beach, because it is so beautiful to gaze at and explore. However, this is a place where sand storms are not uncommon during very windy days. During windless days, Polihua Beach is ideal for sunbathing, picnicking, and photo opportunities. But remember, never go to Polihua

Beach if you intend to go swimming, since Polihua Beach is completely exposed to the open ocean with no protective reef or rocks at all. With its usual strong currents, it might easily sweep you out to sea, even on a calm day. So, never get deceived by the calm looks of Polihua Beach.

Pali Le No Haunai Lookout

Go to the western side of Manele Bay and you will not miss the Pali Le No Haunai Lookout, which is truly a remarkable sight to behold. From Pali Le NO Haunai Lookout, you can see beautiful sea cliffs protecting the bay against strong currents and high surf, making it a natural romantic destination, with countless people making it a point to visit this spot for a great scrutiny of the Pacific. Visitors can view the beautiful sea cliffs from several angles, but the most beautiful sight comes looking out from New Manele Road near Manele Golf Course.

Garden of the Gods

Garden of the Gods is another truly must-see unique, eerie, and mostly dry and often windy tourist destination where beautiful and interesting rock formations were shaped by thousands of years of erosion. It has been said that the rocks and boulders in this specific spot were dropped from the sky by the gods nurturing their gardens, thus the name Garden of the Gods. If you want to see its beauty at its best, come early morning or late evening when the sun's energy hits the minerals in the rock and bring out their most dynamic colors of wonderful purple and red.

This spot, Garden of the Gods, is situated just 7 miles from downtown Lanai City. To make this 1-hour round trip to visit the site, you must take Highway 440 North out of Lanai City passing by the Lodge at Koele. As soon as you see a rock sign on the right side of the road, take that road and turn left on Polihua Road between the tennis courts and the horse stables. Make a right turn at the next intersection and continue driving north-west to the site. Only 4-wheel drive vehicles are allowed on this dirt road, but you may also check with the rental car companies if this road is open before deciding to travel by car on it. And should you do so, make sure your gas tank is full since the site is a very remote area, with little or no gas stations at all. Also, don't fail to bring snacks and drinks as you will not see any convenience stores along the way.

The Local Gentry

Don't forget to drop by Lanai's Local Gentry, Lanai's most charming shop offering the best clothing styles to locals and visitors alike, clothes that the owner Jenna Gentry Majkus, fashionably made herself. Remember, don't leave Lanai Island without shopping for an assortment of Lanai apparel.

Munro Trail

One of the best places to explore in the island of Lanai is the Munro Trail, and for sure it will be one of your most favorite trails in the state. The trail will take you to a tropical rainforest of exactly 3,370 feet, where upon reaching the peak of Lana I'hale on a clear day, you might see all six beautifully astonishing islands in one glance. It's truly an awesome experience to see such a breathtaking landscape from every angle. Make sure to bring your camera with you for once- in-a-lifetime photo opportunities of seeing 6 islands in one day.

Hulopo'e Bay

If there is one beach that is a safe place to swim, it is the Hulopo'e Bay. So, if you have kids with you who are dying to swim on the beautiful beaches of Lanai, bring them to this protected beach composed of beautiful white sands and underwater coral formations the island of Lanai boasts of. It is best that you find lodging at the Manele Bay Hotel as it is overlooking this perfect beach. Other activities you may enjoy doing here include snorkeling, scuba diving, and body surfing. There are also available picnic tables and grills, should you wish to have picnics on this beautiful beach abounding with multi-colored tropical fish and unique coral formations. See how the island of Lanai abounds in breathtaking attractions. If you want to escape the hustle and bustle of your busy life, just run away to this beautiful and untamed part of Lanai

Things to See in Lanai

You'll need an off-road vehicle to reach the sights listed below. Four-wheel-drive rentals on Lanai are expensive.but worth it for a day or two of adventure. For details on vehicle rentals, see "Planning a Trip."

Your first stop on Lanai (perhaps after baptizing yourself at Hulopoe Beach) should be the Lanai Culture & Heritage Center, 730 Lanai Ave. (808/565-7177), located in the heart of town. Orient yourself to the island's cultural and natural history at this tiny, well-curated museum. Learn how indigenous Hawaiians navigated thousands of miles of Pacific Ocean, see relics of the Dole plantation years, and get directions to the island's petroglyph fields. Even better, ask the docents to recount local legends passed down in their families. A visit is guaranteed to make your explorations of Lanai that much richer.

Off the Tourist Trail: Eastside Lanai

If you've got good weather and a trusty 4x4 vehicle, go find adventure on Lanai's untamed east side. Bring snacks and extra water; there are no facilities out here and cell service is scarce. Follow Keomoku Road for 8 miles to the coast. Here the road turns to dirt, mud, or sand; proceed with caution. Head left to find Shipwreck Beach and the Kukui Point petroglyphs.

Venture right to explore a string of empty beaches and abandoned villages, including Keomoku about 5 3/4 miles down the rough-and-tumble dirt road. This former ranching and fishing community of 2,000 was home to the first non-Hawaiian settlement on Lanai. A ghost town since the mid-1950s, it dried up after droughts killed off the Maunalei Sugar Company. Check out Ka Lanakila, the sweetly restored church that dates back to 1903.

Continue another 2 miles to the deserted remains of Club Lanai. A lonely pier stretches into the Pacific from a golden-sand beach populated by coconut palms, a few gazebos, and an empty bar floating in a lagoon. You can pretend you're on the set of *Gilligan's Island* here. This secluded area's Hawaiian name, Halepaloa, means "whale ivory house." Historians speculate that the teeth and bones of a sperm whale rare in these waters once washed ashore here. If you have time, press on to Lopa Beach (good for surfing, not for swimming). The road ends at Naha Beach with its ancient fishponds. Return the way you came and take any trash with you.

Keahiakawelo (Garden of the Gods)
A four-wheel-drive dirt road leads out of Lanai City, through fallow pineapple fields, past the Kanepuu Preserve (see below) to Keahiakawelo. The rugged beauty of this place is punctuated by boulders

strewn by volcanic forces and sculpted by the elements into varying shapes and colors brilliant reds, oranges, ochers, and yellows.

Modern visitors nicknamed this otherworldly landscape "the Garden of the Gods," but its ancient Hawaiian name, Ke-ahi-a-kawelo, means "the fire of Kawelo." According to legend, it's the site of a sorcerers' battle. Kawelo, a powerful *kahuna* (priest) noticed that the people and animals of Lanai were falling ill. He traced their sickness to smoke coming from the neighboring island of Molokai. There, an ill-intentioned priest, Lanikaula, sat chanting over a fire. Kawelo started a fire of his own, here at Keahiakawelo, and tossed some of Lanikaula's excrement into the flames. The smoke turned purple, Lanikaula perished, and health and prosperity returned to Lanai.

Take the dusty, bumpy drive out to Keahiakewalo early in the morning or just before sunset, when the light casts eerie shadows on the mysterious lava formations. Drive west from Koele Lodge on Polihua Road; in about 2 miles, you'll see a hand-painted sign pointing left down a one-lane, red-dirt road through a *kiawe* forest to the large stone sign. Don't stack rocks or otherwise disturb this interesting site; leave everything as you found it.

Munro Trail

In the first golden rays of dawn, when owls swoop silently over the abandoned pineapple fields, take a peek at Mount Lanaihale, the 3,370-foot summit of Lanai. If it's clear, hop into a 4x4 and head for the Munro Trail, the narrow, winding ridge trail that runs across Lanai's razorback spine to its peak. From here, you may get a rare treat: On a clear day, you can see most of the main islands in the Hawaiian chain.

But if it's raining, forget it. On rainy days, the Munro Trail becomes slick and boggy with major washouts. Rainy-day excursions often end with a rental jeep on the hook of the island's lone tow truck and a $250 tow charge. You could even slide off into a major gulch and never be found, so don't try it. But in late August and September, when trade winds stop blowing and the air over the islands stalls in what's called a *kona*condition, Mount Lanaihale's suddenly visible summit becomes an irresistible attraction.

Look for a red-dirt road off Manele Road (Hwy. 440), about 5 miles south of Lanai City; turn left and head up the ridgeline. No sign marks the peak, so you'll have to keep an eye out. Look for a wide spot in the road and a clearing that falls sharply to the sea. From here you can also see silver domes of Space City atop the summit of Haleakala on Maui; Puu Moaulanui, the tongue-twisting summit of Kahoolawe; the tiny crescent of Molokini; and, looming above the clouds, Mauna Kea on the Big Island. At another clearing farther along the thickly forested ridge, all of Molokai, including the 4,961-foot summit of Kamakou and the faint outline of Oahu (more than 30 miles across the sea), are visible. For details on hiking the trail, see "Hiking & Camping" under "Active Pursuits."

Perfect for a Rainy Day: Lanai Art Center

A perfect activity for a rainy day in Lanai City is the Lanai Art Center, 339 Seventh St., located in the heart of the small town. Top artists from across Hawaii frequently visit this homegrown art program and teach a variety of classes, ranging from raku (Japanese pottery), silk printing, silk screening, pareu making (creating your own design on this islanders' wrap), gyotaku (printing a real fish on your own T-shirt), and watercolor drawing to a variety of other island crafts. The cost for the

2- to 3-hour classes is usually in the $15 to $70 range (materials are extra). For information, call 808/565-7503 .

Luahiwa Petroglyph Field

Lanai is second only to the Big Island in its wealth of prehistoric rock art, but you'll have to search a little to find it. Some of the best examples are on the outskirts of Lanai City, on a hillside site known as Luahiwa Petroglyph Field. The characters incised on 13 boulders in this grassy 3-acre knoll include a running man, a canoe, turtles, and curly-tailed dogs (a latter-day wag put a leash on one).

To get here, take Manele Road from Lanai City toward Hulopoe Beach. About 2 miles out of town, you'll see a pump house on the left. Look up on the hillside for a cluster of dark boulders the petroglyphs are there, but you'll have to zigzag to get to them. Two dirt roads lead off of Manele

Road, on either side of the pump house. Take the first one, which leads straight toward the hillside. After about 1 mile, you'll come to a fork. Head right. Drive for another 1/2 mile. At the first V in the road, take a sharp left and double back the way you came, this time on an upper road. After about 1/4 mile; you'll come to the large cluster of boulders on the right. It's just a short walk up the cliffs (wear walking or hiking shoes) to the petroglyphs. Exit the same way you came. Go between 3pm and sunset for ideal viewing and photo ops. Don't touch the petroglyphs or climb on the rocks; these cultural resources are very fragile.

Kaunolu Village

Out on Lanai's nearly vertical, Gibraltar-like sea cliffs is an old royal compound and fishing village. Now a national historic landmark and one of Hawaii's most treasured ruins, it's believed to have been inhabited by King Kamehameha the Great and hundreds of his closest followers about 200 years ago.

It's a hot, dry, 3-mile 4x4 drive from Lanai City to Kaunolu, but the mini-expedition is worth it. Take plenty of water, don a hat for protection against the sun, and wear sturdy shoes. Signs explain the sacred site's importance. Ruins of 86 house platforms and 35 stone shelters have been identified on both sides of Kaunolu Gulch. The residential complex also includes the Halulu Heiau temple, named after a mythical man-eating bird. The king's royal retreat is thought to have stood on the eastern edge of Kaunolu Gulch, overlooking the rocky shore facing Kahekili's Leap. Chiefs leapt from the 62-foot-high perch as a show of bravado. Nearby are burial caves, a fishing shrine, a lookout tower, and warriorlike stick figures petroglyphs carved on boulders. Just offshore stands the telltale fin of little Shark Island, a popular dive spot that teems with bright tropical fish and, frequently, sharks.

From Lanai City, take Kaumalapau Highway past the airport. Look for a carved boulder on the left side of the road. Turn left onto a dirt road (Kaupili Rd.) and drive east until you see another carved boulder. Turn right, toward the ocean. *Tip:* On your way out, turn right to continue on Kaupili Road. It meets with Hulopoe Drive, a shortcut to Manele Bay.

Kanepuu Preserve

This ancient grove on Lanai's western plateau is the island's last remaining dryland forest, containing 48 native species. A self-guided hike allows visitors to see the rare trees and shrubs that once covered the dry lowlands of all the main Hawaiian Islands. Elsewhere these species have succumbed to axis deer, agriculture, or "progress." The botanical marvels growing within this protected reserve include *olopua* (Hawaiian olive), *lama* (Hawaiian ebony), *maʻo hau hele* (a Hawaiian hibiscus), and *nānū* (Hawaiian gardenia). Kanepuu is easily reached via 4WD. Head west from Koele Lodge on Polihua Road; in about 1 3/4 miles, you'll see the fenced area on the left

Tourist Attractions and Festivals in Lanai

Known as Hawaii's "most exciting island," Lanai is the perfect place for anyone who wants to bask in the charm and intimacy of this small and quaint paradise. From breathtaking landscapes to awe-inspiring seas, Lanai offers you not only a place to admire, but also a place to enjoy fun and exciting adventures (both outdoors and indoors). Although the island itself is considered to be relatively small, it is certainly not limited in terms of outdoor activities. Spanning 89,000 acres of countryside, Lanai still retains a wild and virgin environment that is simply waiting to be explored and discovered by you.

Dole Park

Because the weather in Lanai is relatively dry, this makes your trip to the island perfect for an old-fashioned picnic on the lush greenery. Dole Park is found in the center of Lanai, which serves as the ultimate spot for you to open your picnic basket, lay down a blanket, take your dog for a walk, and maybe even toss around a Frisbee. Filled with tall pine trees and crisp, cool breeze, Dole Park is the ideal destination for anyone who is seeking a free and relaxing activity amidst the beauty of Lanai's nature.

Hulopoe Bay

If you're yearning for the feeling of sand between your toes and the soothing sound of water brushing against the shore, Hulopoe Bay is the perfect place for you. Located in the southern coast of Lanai, Hulopoe Bay is considered one of the best beaches the US has to offer. This is because the bay is protectedmeaning, it is perfect for snorkeling, swimming, boarding, and exploring with its expanse of golden sand and deep blue waters. Aside from this, Hulopoe Bay also has a great beach park, which accommodates you with pretty picnic tables, barbecue grills, comfort rooms, and showers.

Kanepuu Preserve

Located on the west of Lanai, Kanepuu Preserve is the ideal destination for the nature lover in you. Because this rare and beautiful forest is protected by the Nature Conservancy, it contains the remnants of Olopua or Lama dryland forest in all of

Hawaii. Encompassing 590 acres and home to more than 40 native species of plants, Kanepuu Preserve offers you a once-in-a-lifetime opportunity to view one of the Earth's most fragile ecosystems. In order to get around this land of lush greenery, Kanepuu Preserve offers self-guiding maps (for those who want to find their own way through the forest), as well as group tours (where a guided hike is run by the Nature Conservancy of Hawaii).

Kaunolu

In case you've ever wondered what it was like to be Hawaii's King Kamehameha, this is your chance to find out. Deriving his name from the phrase "the lonely one," King Kamehameha was said to have retreated here, in Kaunolu, to find peace and relaxation. Perfect for those who love to go fishing, as well as those who simply want to enjoy an outdoor tour, Kaunolu is less than an hour-drive from Lanai City. Expect serenity atop a high sea cliff with the sweeping whisper of sea and sky all around you, as the beauty of Kaunolu offers peace and solitude.

Keahiakawelo

Known as the Garden of the Gods, Keahiakawelo promises you a trip that will make you forget you're still on Earth. This is because it is a rock garden found at the end of Polihua Road, where the most unique and eerie rocks actually resemble Mars'. In Hawaiian folklore, this landscape is believed to be the result of a competition between two priests who were both challenged to keep a fire burning. The reward was a great abundance of rocks to keep the winner's fire eternally burning. Perfect for picture-taking and exquisitely laid out for anyone seeking artistic inspiration, Keahiakawelo is one of Lanai's most popular tourist attractions.

Lauhiwa Petroglyphs

The Lauhiwa Petroglyphs presents ancient carvings in stone created by the ancient Hawaiians. If you are a history-lover, or simply someone who wants to experience the best of Hawaiian history, this place is ideal for you. With fragile rock drawings that have been spared by the erosion of wet weather, Lanai's Lauhiwa offers one of the most preserved petroglyphs. Because these stone markings are the remnants of Hawaiian culture, visitors are always left in awe by the amazement of these old century relics. With circle patterns, dogs, bird's head, warriors, families and horses, these ancient works of art are a must-see for anyone who wants to fully appreciate the history and culture of Hawaii.

The Munro Trail

Perfect for historic hiking, driving and biking trails, the Munro Trail is located not very far from Lanai proper. Getting its name from George Munro (the naturalist from New Zealand), this one-lane dirt road that spans seven miles gives you sweeping views amidst beautiful pine trees, which were planted by Munro himself. Offering remarkable views and a 1,600-foot climb, the stunning canyon views of Maunalei Gulch and Maui are only the icing on top of the cake. The trail can lead you to the top of Mount Lanaihale, which is Lanai's highest peek at 3,368 feet. Expect to be blown away by the view, the breeze, and the sight of serenity.

The Shipwreck Beach

Shipwreck Beach features ruins of an old lighthouse. Windy, warm, and incredibly romantic, this eight-mile stretch of beach has wrecked and ruined numerous ships along its shallow and rocky channel. Because of this, the place delivers an air of mystery and mystique. Offering breathtaking views of Molokai and Maui, this land is specially perfect for beach-combing and exploration adventures.

The art galleries of Lanai

While strolling the quiet, calm, and cool streets of Lanai, you might want to drop by some of its art galleries, which offer more than just art. Some of these galleries have gift and souvenir shops where you can buy artistic presents for your loved ones, as well as engage in conversations with Lanai's local artists and art patrons. The artists of Lanai are said to be incredibly accommodating as they are warm, friendly, and very open-minded people.

The much-awaited festivals of Lanai

The Pineapple Festival
The Pineapple Festival takes place in Lanai as an occasion to celebrate the land's pineapple plantation and ranch history. Expect abundant amounts of delicious and mouth-watering local

food, as well as crafts-making activities and games. Prepare yourself for some crazy dancing, singing, socializing, and a whole lot more.

The Aloha Festival

This festival is a premiere cultural celebration of Hawaii's local music, dance, art, and history. Expect it to spell out fun and excitement as Hawaii shows you why Lanai is truly one of its most enticing islands. From street parties and food fairs to dance events and local parades, this festival is open to everyone, young and old. Expect hours of fun and excitement.

The Ocean Arts Festival

Between November and May, hundreds of Humpback Whales migrate to the waters around Hawaii. Due to the warm and shallow conditions, they are drawn between the islands of Maui and Lanai, where it is ideal for whales to mate and give birth. Because of this, these whales have become celebrities in Hawaii. Witness moments when traveling vehicles actually stop their engines, with the sight of the whales passing by the waters. For the same reason, tons of artists come to the island to witness the view of the whales and to create their own whale- and ocean-inspired artworks. Similarly, musicians and Hula troops perform regularly, while naturalists give free talks on the lives of Humpback Whales.

The International Film Festival

Every year, the International Film Festival comes to Hawaii to showcase only the finest films that the world has to offer. Instead of heading to movie theaters, you can simply stay outdoors to enjoy the films that are screened for free. You can also avail of a tour of the beautiful night sky, where an astrologer explains the meanings behind every star. In addition to all of these, the festival also includes art talks on the craft of movie-making, as well as musical and dance performances inspired by the movies themselves. Expect the Lanai Theater to offer the best of the events that this wonderful festival has to offer.

The Lei Day Festival

Because of Hawaii's perfectly sunny and crisp weather in May, Hawaii celebrates the Lei Day by holding beauty pageants in schools, as well as lei dance performances and competitions. Adults are asked to wear and give out leis to their loved ones. For this reason, you can say that the Lei Day Festival is somewhat a form of Valentine's Day in Hawaii, where the warm and inviting expression of love and beauty is shared with one another.

The Christmas Festival and Tree-Lighting Ceremony

In December, Lanai celebrates the Christmas Festival and Tree-Lighting Ceremony where you can expect an abundance of Christmas music, dance parties, and even heartwarming theatrical plays and performances. Topping it all off is the Tree-Lighting Ceremony, where everyone is invited to come and witness the lighting of Lanai's magical, beautiful, ands grand Christmas tree.

Cuisine of Lanai

Lanai is one of smallest islands of Hawaii. But even though it is less developed than the other islands, it has much to offer to visiting tourists. Lanai does possess a certain charm that makes it the island of choice of many city dwellers and adventure travelers. Bill Gates, for one, chose Lanai to be the venue of his wedding in 1994. Perhaps the world-famous billionaire found the privacy and serenity he wanted for celebrating a special day in his life. The same is true for people from around the world who come to visit Lanai all-year round to spend vacation, take part in festivals, and hold their weddings. It's not called the "The Secluded Island" for no reason at all.

Here in Lanai, you won't find any traffic light or endless stretch of paved road. Instead, you'll be surrounded by lush greenery and sandy beaches, which serve as a good backdrop for oceanfront dining that's popular in the island. Aside from the friendliness of the people, the spectacular view of the ocean and mountain peaks, dining here in Lanai is something to look forward to. With its wide array of dishes and mix of culinary influences, it is in Lanai where you'll get a true taste of Pacific Rim flavors.

Hawaiian dining

You'd probably think that because of the rich soils of Hawaii, it was fairly easy for them to infuse new flavors to their dishes using the local ingredients.

But the gustatory delights Hawaii is known for were not made overnight. There was even a time when locals mostly enjoyed packed food that came from the US. Popular treats back then were frozen pizza and its world-famous pineapple. But as time went by and as tourists soon flock to the islands of Hawaii, local dining only became more exciting. Different ingredients were grown to add new and fresh flavors to their homegrown recipes. The plantation days also brought in different culinary recipes from the Philippines, Korea, Japan, and even Portugal.

It is here in Hawaii where you'll find a good mix of traditional oriental cooking and dishes from the Western world. From these, they infused their own styles of cooking and tried to diversify by adding new flavors that are native to the island. These specialties are commonly served in the famous luaus and Hawaiian festivals. There are also local diners and beachfront restaurants that offer a wide array of Hawaiian dishes in their menu. Today, Hawaii is not just known for its sweet pineapples but also for its Pacific Rim flavors that were cultivated over the years.

Dishes in Lanai

Here in Lanai, poi remains to be a staple food, commonly served in luaus and even as ordinary home meal. It is a sticky purple paste made from the taro plant. Poi actually plays a big role in their culture. It is said that with poi on the table, people around it should not engage in any fight or argument. This is because poi is a symbol used to represent the ancestor of chiefs and the native Hawaiians.

The people of Lanai also carry the tradition of roasting pig during special occasions. The inhabitants of this island also takes advantage of the rich marine life. Many of their cuisines are actually prepared using seafood. Locals take pride in their seafood specialties. These dishes are sprinkled with just the right herbs, spices, and other ingredients to add flavor to fresh catches.

The native Hawaiian dishes are just part of the island's cuisine. Like everything else in Lanai, many cuisines have been influenced by diverse cultures. In this island, you can actually sample various types of dishes, from native Hawaiian, European, and Japanese to the fusion of all these.

If you're in for a week-long vacation in Lanai, you'll have all the time you need to dine in all its restaurants. There are just a little over 10 restaurants here. While some of the dining estalibshments are downright luxurious, some are just right even for a tight budget. In any of these restaurants, you'll surely receive the gift of the "aloha" spirit from its service crew.

Fist-class restaurants in Lanai

The two major resorts in the island can offer you a fine dining experience. Lodge at Koele's Formal Dining Room and Manele Bay Hotel's Ihilani Restaurant are both listed in Gourmet Magazine as among the best restaurants in Hawaii. Lodge at Koele's Fomarl Dining Room serves mostly American cuisines, while the Ihilani Restaurant of Manele Bay Hotel offers French cuisine. Here in Ihilani, you have the poached lobster, foie gras, and Porcini mushroom soup as among your menu choices. Both Ihilani and The Lodge at Koele require formal wear.

Henry Clay's Rotisserie in Hotel Lanai is also one of the best restaurants in the island that serve American cuisine. Among the culinary specialties of this establishment are seafood dishes and rotisserie meats. Henry Clay's Rotisserie is also acclaimed for its pecan pie. Compared to the above-mentioned restaurants, Henry Clay's Rotisserie has a more laid-back ambiance.

The Terrace Restaurant of Lodge at Koele offers American cuisine as well. The menu includes burger, salads, and sandwiches. while dining in this place, you can watch the beautiful garden and pine forests through its glass walls.

The Challenge at Manele Clubhouse is best known for its fish tacos, ahi sashimi, and Chinese barbecued chicken salad. This restaurant provides a nice view of the Pacific Ocean. If you want to try a combination of various cuisines, you should visit Hulopoe Court, which is found in the Four Seasons Resort at Manele Bay. This restaurant has received accolades for its Pacific Rim seafood dishes. Aside from serving sumptuous cuisines, it also offers excellent oceanview from every table.

Restaurants with laid-back atmosphere

Pele's Other Garden is another recommended dining place in Lanai. It offers gourmet deli, from sandwiches and pizzas to many more delectable snacks. Pele's Other Garden can provide you with a picnic basket if you want to tour around the place. The best thing about this dining place is that it transforms into an Italian Bistro by night.

If you want a poolside dining experience, Ocean Grille is an ideal choice for you. Here, you can dine during or after you dip in the water. This tropical bar provides drinks and smoothies, salads, burgers, and sandwiches, among other island specials. This establishment is popular for its basket of taro chips.

You can also enjoy a more laid-back ambiance in Blue Ginger Cafe. Its menu includes spam, egg, burgers, sandwiches, and Portuguese sausages. You can also opt to have your juicy burgers from Tanigawa's. Here, you'll surely enjoy meat dishes. If you want to sample a blend of Lanai's ethnic and local cuisines you can go to Cafe 565, which serves pizza, salads, and sandwiches. If you are fond of ice creams, you should not miss the Sweetest Days Ice Cream, where you can buy scoops of your favorite ice cream flavor and other desserts.

If you want to experience the famous luau or the traditional party of the Hawaiians, you can make arrangements with the Four Seasons Resort Lanai at Manele Bay.

Most of the restaurants in Lanai do not have delivery services, so you really have to go to the restaurants to have your meal. It would be worth it because the dishes are not the only things to look forward to, you'll also enjoy the view, the ambiance, and service from the friendly staff who are always ready with their smiles. Many of the establishments are located in beach front, where you will surely have a view of the clear waters, powdery sands, and tropical trees.

Remember to make reservations in fine dining restaurants to get a good seat and ensure accommodation. In restaurants for middle-class budget, there is no need for you to dress up formally. You can just wear anything comfortable.

Food booths

During festivals, there are also cooking contests where you will see how people prepare different cuisines. Aside from this, there are lots of booths that sell food and beverages. If you attend the Pineapple Festival, for instance, you can sample the different dishes from these booths. During Lanai's Aloha Festival, you will also find food stations that serve Hawaiian favorites. What's great about this experience is that you will get the chance to mingle with the locals and tourists alike. This is a good opportunity for you to hear their stories and travel experiences.

Your dining experience in Lanai won't be complete if you miss the island's local cuisine. You have to include in your itinerary restaurants that serve local favorites. Budget don't have to be much of a problem. There are lots of restaurants in this island that offer excellent Lanaian cuisines without burning a hole in your pocket.

Other than good-tasting food, there are a lot of things to make your dining experience in Lanai memorable. The magnificent view of the beach and the lush greenery in the island would also whet your appetite. Another essential part of the Lanaian dining experience is the warm welcome and the hospitality of the people.

Manele Bay, Lanai

Manele Bay is located in the southern coast of Lanai. This beautiful place is divided into two: White Manele and Black Manele. As part of the Marine Life Conservation District, visitors of Manele Bay are asked to take part in the conservation practices. There are so many beautiful places to explore in Manele Bay. Explore the lush greeneries, crystal clear blue waters, and sandy beaches amidst spectacular views of Lanai's coastline.

White Manele or Hulopoe Bay
At White Manele, or Hulopoe Bay, you will find one of America's best beaches – Hulopoe Beach. The beach is famous for its golden sand and deep

blue waters which will definitely entice you to swim, snorkel, sunbathe, or simply relax with family and friends.

Hulopoe Bay is Lanai's best location for body boarding, snorkeling, and swimming. The place is also frequented by locals and tourists because of the spinner dolphins and humpback whales that are usually seen here. Because Hulopoe Bay is part of the marine life conservation district, you will find the place as one of the best spots for snorkeling and diving. The abundance of marine life will definitely take your breath away.

At Hulopoe Beach, you will also find facilities like picnic tables, restrooms, barbecue grills, and shower rooms. As a protected site, visitors are asked to help in preserving the beauty of the place.

Hulopoe tide pools

At the east side of the bay, you will find the famous Hulopoe tide pools. The calm clear blue waters and abundant marine life here also attract many visitors. The changing tides – high and low tides – created these tide pools. During high tide, the rocky shores are covered by water. But during low tide, these are exposed. Here you will find hermit crabs, small fish, and sea stars. The pools' calm waters make this a perfect place for exploring. Just be very cautious because the rocks can get really slippery.

Shark's Cove
Another great place to explore in Manele Bay is the Shark's Cove or Shark's Bay. This secluded beach is popular for its red lava rock formation. On top of the lava rock, you will get magnificent views of Lanai's breathtaking coastline. The sandy beach and clear waters are great to enjoy some privacy while reading a book or relaxing by the shore.

Puu Pehe Rock

Puu Pehe Rock, or Sweetheart Rock, is the stunning 80-foot rock seen about 150 feet off the shore. On top of the rock is an ancient structure believed to be part of a Hawaiian legend about a couple. According to the legend, a lovely girl named Pehe lived with her husband in the sea caves. One day, while the husband was away, a very strong storm came to the island. When the husband returned, he was anguished to see his wife's lifeless body. He climbed the 150-foot rock and buried his wife on top of it. Then, the husband jumped off the rock to kill himself. Another popular name for the rock formation is Lover's Leap. The cove at Puu Pehe Rock has clear blue waters and abundant marine life as well.

Black Manele

On this side of Manele Bay, you will find the boat harbor. The harbor is surrounded by sea cliffs known as the Pali Lei noHauni. Aside from protecting the harbor from strong storms, the sea cliffs also provide magnificent views of the bay.

Golf Course

If you are a golf enthusiast, you will definitely love to visit and play at the famous golf course in Manele Bay – The Challenge at Manele. This oceanside course will give you majestic views of the ocean. Found at the luxurious Manele Bay Resort, The Challenge at Manele is a 72-par championship golf course. Unveiled in December 1993, the golf course was designed by Jack Nicklaus who also designed the famous Experience at Koele.

Located on top of a 200-foot lava sea cliff, the golf course has 18 holes, a driving range, a pro shop, a putting green, and a clubhouse.

Four Seasons Resort

Lanai Island, Hawaii. USA

A famous 5-star luxurious resort, the Four Seasons Resort, has breathtaking ocean views, peaceful tropical beaches, and the best accommodation that Manele Bay has to offer. If you stay here, it is like having a piece of Hawaii's paradise all to yourself. Four Seasons Resort is situated in a secluded area along Manele Bay, which offers a lot of privacy for its guests.

The resort has maintained the natural and breathtaking beauty of its beaches and lush greeneries. Spinner dolphins and humpback whales are usually seen at a distance when in season.

If you want a stress-free vacation that is far from the noise of city life, the Four Seasons Resort is the best place for you. Its relaxing atmosphere, serene and pristine beaches with crystal clear blue waters will definitely make you feel rejuvenated. From the resort, you can have spectacular views of Kaho'olawe and Maui. You might even see the Big Islands from a distance on a clear day.

The resort has 236 spacious guest rooms with garden or ocean views. Each room has a private lanai which has a small dining table with two chairs and a daybed. Amenities in every room include dual-line telephones with voice mail, 40-inch LCD television, rattan writing desk, DVD player, and high-speed Internet access.

During your stay at the resort, you can enjoy the following recreational activities: guided tour of the resort gardens; exercise at the fitness center with state-of-the-art cardiovascular equipment; fitness classes like yoga, spinning, water aerobics, and Pilates at the Movement Studio; entertainment and video games at the Surf Shack Teen Center which has PlayStation 2 consoles; foosball, pool, darts, or shuffleboard at the Games Room. Aside from all these, there's snorkeling gear, a putting green, tennis equipment, and a swimming pool with 2 whirlpools.

There are still so many things to do at the Four Seasons Resort. Because of its proximity to Hulopoe Bay, you can enjoy many water sports activities like deep-sea fishing and snorkeling.

There are also many land activities that you can enjoy. One is hiking. There are many fascinating and scenic routes to choose from. You can also go horseback riding across the beautiful landscapes.

If you have children that are 5 to 12 years old, you need not worry that they will run out of things to do at the resort. The Four Seasons Resort has a Kids For All Seasons Program called the Pilialoha Keiki Camp. The program offers different indoor and outdoor activities for children.

Day and night activities are both offered. Some of the daytime activities that your children will surely enjoy are exploring the tidal pools while learning about sea creatures, hiking through the Manele Bay Gardens, and creating things through the arts and crafts classes. And in the evening, your children can go stargazing, singing and join and a karaoke contest, hunting for sand crabs or geckos, and many more.

If you want to simply relax and rejuvenate your body, head off to the resort's spa and choose among its many different massages, body treatments, and spa services.

The Four Seasons Resort was designed for the entire family. Young and old alike will have a grand time at the resort. And it has the best location for an unforgettable family vacation.

Are you planning on visiting Lanai, Hawaii's most enticing island? Do not forget to explore these majestic places in Manele Bay. Just remember that the place is a conservation site. You can definitely find beautiful and breathtaking views. But you must help out in preserving its natural beauty. Don't take rocks or plants as souvenirs and make sure to not leave any trash behind. Enjoy your stay at Manele Bay and preserve its beauty at the same time.

Manele Bay, Lanai on a Budget

Manele Bay is the place you would like to go to even if you are on a budget. It is a notable place since it has a beautiful harbor that is open to the public. If you want to get there from Maui, the public harbor is where you will first set your foot on in the island Lanai. Some beaches in Lanai are accessible only by 4-wheel drives, and for a good reason. Just a glimpse at the island will give you an idea what paradise looks like. Its seemingly endless line of white sands bordered by clear blue waters on one side and green landscape on the other makes you feel that you want to lie there forever. The place has a tropical climate and you can expect the sun to shine brightly each day. The island is surrounded by tranquil blue waters and clear skies above, making it an ideal place to relax. This is the island to go to if you want to break free from all the haste and noise of your corporate life.

If you are on a budget, Manele Bay can offer you a relaxing place to enjoy your Hawaiian cruise. At the end of the bay, you will find a white sand beach that stretches on the east side of the island. The beach might be smaller compared to the rest of the commercial beaches on the island, but it is enough to soothe your senses. It still has the tranquil, tropical aura which the island offers to its visitors. The place is also a perfect spot to explore the wonders under the Hawaiian sea. Many tourists visit the place to enjoy snorkeling. If you can be looser with your budget, you may try diving in the bay. It means additional cost but what you will see are wonders that cannot be found anywhere else.

Transportation costs
You can travel directly from Honolulu to Lanai City by taking a short flight. A plane trip price for a single person depends on the season and the airline carrier. Aside from a one-way trip ticket, you can arrange for a round trip ticket. Plane companies usually give discount for round trip and group packages. The accommodation for a cheap plane ticket is economy but the service is among the finest that you can have for that class. If you are already in Maui or Oahu, you can reach the island by taking a boat trip. You will be engaging in

an enjoyable tour as you cruise your way to the bay. You can make your reservations online to know more about the exact cost of the trip. You can also find out about the details of the trip online. If you want to have more fun on your way to Manele Bay, book for a boat trip that goes around the island of Lanai. You can still enjoy an island-round cruise even if you are on a budget since trip packages are also available.

Once you get there
Most likely, the first thing that you will do when you get to Manele Bay is take pictures of just about everything around you. You cannot help it. The place is just too beautiful to miss a single detail. Everything that you will set your eyes upon will charm you. But you cannot stay on the bay for the rest of your trip. You must find a place to stay first. There is one near Manele Bay but you may not find the price easy on your budget. This means

that you will have to go to Lanai City to find accommodation. You must have a place to leave your things so you can enjoy Manele Bay to the utmost. You will not find the trip exhausting as the city is only eight miles away from the beach. Rooms in luxury resorts are quite costly, considering that the island is an elite vacation place. Most of the time, the rates here are over $500 per night. Of course, you do not want to spend that much money for a single evening's accommodation only. Fortunately, there are rooms which cost a hundred dollars or less. Usually, these rooms do not come with a meal package but that shouldn't be a problem. Anyway, you can find delectable tropical food all over the city, especially in the evening.

A shuttle is the ideal vehicle to ride from Manele Bay to Lanai. If you are on a package, the fare should no longer be a deal. However, if the case is otherwise, then you may just opt for a cab. On a cab, you can get basically anywhere in the island. Some find it more fun to rent bicycles and you can do this as well. Rates vary from one rental agency to another. You can easily inquire for the price once you get to the city.

Fun and affordable activities in Manele Bay
You will never get tired of boat trips when you are touring the Hawaiian Islands. That is why you should know about another exciting trip that you may want to have: a boat trip to Puu Pehe. Puu Pehe is just across Manele Bay, and you can even see the bay's lone hotel when you are there. You will also be presented with a stunning view of the Hulopo'e Beach Park as you cruise your way around the huge stone wonder.

If you want to enjoy golfing, you have just gotten lucky. Manele Bay is famous for one golf course which blends the corporate sports with extreme adventure: The Challenge at Manele. For $190, you can play your heart out at one of the most challenging and ingenious golf courses in the planet.

Of course, snorkeling and diving are still some of the most popular activities in the bay. The myriads of colors hidden beneath the clear blue waters of the bay are just so enchanting. The wonders beneath the sea just never grow old. Make sure that you bring your diving suit along so you will not have to rent. It will also help if you bring all the snorkeling devices that you might need. As long as they do not cause much inconvenience, it is better to bring all that you will need to save all the money you can.

Enjoying the trip while saving money
Going to Manele and staying there naturally costs a lot. However, you can still save if you plan your trip well. Do some research before going to the

island. Know the most affordable hotels to stay. Find out about some affordable dining places. The Hawaii Travel Bureau can provide you with information on how you can save on your trip.

When you are already in Lanai, you must keep in mind that everything that you pay there is greater that what you would normally pay in other places. Therefore, you must be prudent with your spending. Try to decide whether you should buy something or not. As for the car rentals, it cannot be avoided if you want to make the most of your island trip. Just be sure that you are paying for the right cars. Do not settle for the first rental company that offers you a deal. Know what is in store for you out there. You might still be able to get better prices.

Also, do not rent cars without having a plan on where to go to. It would be best to take the shuttle or a cab on your way to Manele Bay from Lanai as it is much cheaper. But should you inevitably overspend, worry about your money later; there is still a paradise to be enjoyed.

How to Get to Manele Bay, Lanai

Manele Bay is a stunning paradox crafted by the unseen hands of nature. The island is where you can have the best of both rugged mountains and clear blue beach waters. A view from the air will reveal to you the vast green forestry and grass planes which cover much of the island. Between the blue waters and the white shores are sea foams which define the boundary between land and sea. Much of the coastline in Manele Bay is covered by sharp rocks and sands. However, this does not render the place less beautiful. The short strip of public beach along the bay is all that you will need to experience paradise for free. There you can lie on the sand while the cool Hawaiian breeze gently passes by. There are also several public places in the bay where you can meet interesting tourists. The Manele Sitting room is where you will meet some of the nicest tourists you will ever come across. You will surely experiences all these thrills and wonders once you get to Manele Bay. Now all you have to know is how to get there.

From Honolulu via plane
There are several means to get to Manele Bay. All this depends on where your starting point is. If your starting point is the island of Honolulu, you can travel through a 40-seater plane operated by a company called Island Air. Their plane will land you in the City of Lanai where a small airport is located. Flights are scheduled every two or three hours so it is best to know the schedules first as you do not want to spend time waiting at the airport. There

are also other plane companies that you can fly with. One is Go! Express. They offer discount packages just like Pacific Wings. Pacific Wings is another airline company that can take you to Lanai at low costs.

Whichever plane you will take, you will be landing at Puuwai Basin. The trip between Honolulu and Lanai usually takes 30 minutes. When you are already there, you can find a shuttle which will take you to the City of Lanai. Puuwai Basin is not far from the city so you should expect your trip to be just about ten minutes. From the city, you can start your trip to Manele Bay at whatever transportation that you prefer. You can rent motorbikes or ATVs or a car. You can also take a taxi from there should you prefer that. The bay is just eight miles from the city so you do not have to worry about a long trip. If you go directly from

Puuwai Basin to Manele Bay, the trip will take you approximately 25 minutes.

Hopping from Maui
If you are in Maui, you can reach Lanai in about 45 minutes through a ferryboat. Less than $30 is all that you will need to cross the channel which stretches 9 miles between Maui and Lanai. You will arrive directly at Manele Bay, a popular tourist spot that's well-known in the entire island. When the sea conditions are not fair, your trip to Lanai may take an hour or more.

Going around the island
Manele Bay is an enchanting place where you can snorkel your way to discovering the undersea wonders of Hawaii. It is a piece of paradise whose memories you will take home with pleasure. If you want to see more places other than the bay, you can go around the island through a jeep. There are rugged plains which can provide you with the Lanai

brand of off-road adventure. Enjoy whatever sight and pleasures you can find in the island as you will find nothing like them in other places

What to Do in Manele Bay, Lanai

Manele Bay, situated at the southern part of Lanai in Hawaii, is a secluded harbour that attracts many tourists and travelers per year. Expedition ferries that transport tourists from Maui to Lanai and vice-versa dock at the harbour of Manele Bay, making the area a convenient stop-over for many travelers planning to explore the rest of Lanai. Whether you are planning to stay at Manele Bay for the rest of your vacation or to spend a few nights at this side Lanai before heading off to discover the rest of the bigger island, there are many things to do and sights to see in this secluded, southern harbour.

The best thing about Manele Bay is that it is a quiet, peaceful place for a vacation. While there are no nightclubs and posh restaurants, the place has a culture and a unique Aloha spirit not found anywhere else. Those who want to experience the finest amenities and sporting activities can head off to the famed Four Seasons Resort Lanai at Manele Bay. However, Manele Bay is beyond luxury, as you can always explore the rest of the area without spending a fortune. Here are the things that you can do while staying at Manele Bay.

Sporting activities at Manele Bay, Lanai
Golf and tennis
If you love playing golf during your vacation, you can check in at the Four Seasons Resort Lanai at Manele Bay and indulge in a game on the world's best golf courses. The golf course at this luxury resort has a spectacular backdrop, fringed by palm

trees, while each hole affords the player a full view of the distant Pacific Ocean. Rental clubs as well as golf instruction are available. During winter months, migrating whales can be sighted on the Pacific, a majestic sight from the resort's well-manicured golf course.

Tennis lovers will also appreciate the top-notch tennis facilities at the Four Seasons Resort Lanai at Manele Bay. Three outdoor courts are available for tennis enthusiasts at the resort, while tennis equipments and outfits are offered as well. For a fee, you can also take tennis lessons, which are available in private settings or in group courses.

Swimming
At Manele Bay you will find the Hulopoe Beach, famed all over the world for its spectacular fine white sand and clear, warm waters. Whether you are staying at the Four Seasons resort or renting

your own Manele Bay condo, you can always enjoy swimming at the Hulopoe bay.

Snorkeling and scuba diving
Manele Bay is divided into two parts, which are the white Manele and the black Manele. The white Manele area is where Hulopoe beach is located. The rich marine life of Hulopoe beach makes it an ideal location for underwater excursions, including snorkeling and scuba diving. Here you will find rare tropical fish species, wondrous coral reef formations, and underwater caverns that bring the underwater scene of Hulopoe Beach to life. If you are checked in at the Four Seasons Resort, you may rent out snorkeling equipment, for a fee.

Hulopoe Bay is also a protected marine reserve, and with an abundance of coral reef formations and colorful marine life, this location is one of the best scuba diving spots in Lanai. Diving excursions are offered to both first-time and experienced divers, and diving gear are available for rent as well.

Surfing and body boarding
Hawaii is known as the surfing Mecca of the world and here at Manele Bay, visitors can take pleasure from exhilarating surfboarding and body boarding activities. Surfing lessons are offered at Manele Bay, where expert surfing instructors can teach you how to ride the waves in top form.

Fishing, sailing, and marine life search excursions
With the diverse marine life of Hulopoe Bay, it is not uncommon to witness spinner dolphins along its seashores, or migrating whales during the winter months. Witnessing the best of Hulopoe Bay marine life is made possible through marine life search excursions offered at the Four Seasons Resort. During idyllic weather, you can also go sailing over the placid waters of Hulopoe bay. Four Seasons Resort also offers organized deep-sea

fishing activities, where you can catch some mahi mahi, yellow fin, or blue marlin.

Camping activities at Manele Bay, Lanai
Budget recreational activities are also available at Manele Bay, Lanai. If you want to enjoy the offerings of this isolated location in Lanai Island without busting your budget, why not engage in a beachside camping activity with your friends and family? Hulopoe Beach Park is a famous camping site at Manele Bay, where campers can rent a camping tent and stay at the beach park after securing the necessary permits.

Here you will be able to enjoy your own private paradise, away from the throng of tourists and beachgoers which crowd the resorts of the more populous Hawaiian Islands. Picnic sites are comfortably sheltered by trees and foliage, while barbeque sites are found scattered among the six camp sites of Hulopoe Beach Park. Comfortable facilities like restrooms and shower rooms can be found at the site, perfect for extended overnight stays or for a day spent swimming and exploring the underwater life of the harbour.

Hiking at Black Manele
Apart from white Manele, where the Hulopoe Beach is found, black Manele is one part that comprises the bigger Manele Bay. The best sights to discover at black Manele are the Pali Lei no Hauni sea cliffs. Although these cliffs provide fortification against strong winds and powerful currents, they also offer anyone a stunning vista of the Pacific Ocean. You can head to New Manele Road to view these amazing sea cliffs, where there are also picnic areas to be found, for longer and more comfortable sightseeing trips.

Explore the rest of Lanai Island
When you're in Manele Bay, you can also take the chance to explore the rest of beautiful Lanai Island.

Lanai is an irresistible combination of stunning coastlines and verdant mountain forests, giving you a vacation experience that is truly Hawaii. Tranquil, unspoiled, and enchanting Lanai offers a host of attractions to curious travelers.

The Lodge at Koele is one of the more famous resort accommodations on the island, along with the Four Seasons Resort Lanai at Manele Bay. The Lodge at Koele has world-class golf courses, state-of-the art fitness center with spa, tennis courts, and well-maintained stables. It also offers a total of 102 well-appointed rooms, including a suite accommodation. Mountain hunting activities are offered at the lodge, too.

Hotel Lanai on the other hand, is an intimate bed and breakfast with only eleven rooms offered to guests. If you want to experience the inland charms of Lanai, you may choose to be billeted at these hotels.

The Lanai Art Center is a haven for those who have a keen eye for art. Here you can view the amazing works of Lanai artists, which include paintings, photographs, sketches, and woodwork creations. Anyone interested in taking up art lessons are welcome here. Whether you intend to learn about traditional Hawaiian arts and crafts or pottery, private lessons can be had at the Lanai Art Center.

Lanai offers some of the best hiking trips, such as the Koloiki Ridge Hike. A 5-mile hike that allows you to enjoy the scenic beauty of the island in seclusion, you will be afforded with spectacular views of the Pacific Ocean, as well as the nearer islands of Maui and Molokai. You can also shop for souvenir items at Lanai City, where souvenir boutiques are found in the area. Stylish island wear and unique gift items are just some of the merchandises you can found in downtown Lanai.

Where to Stay in Manele Bay, Lanai

Manele Bay is one of the most popular destinations in Lanai, the sixth largest island in all of Hawaii. Found on the southernmost tip of Lanai, Manele Bay is known to be the most sheltered of all of the island harbours. This seclusion has made Manele Bay a popular recreational spot for both the locals and visiting tourists. A number of yachts, ferries, and tour vessels are found on the harbour, especially those carrying travelers and passengers between Maui and Lanai.

Royal accommodations at the Four Season's Resort Lanai at Manele Bay

If you're planning a vacation in Lanai, especially in the Manele Bay area, checking in at the Four

Season's Resort Lanai at Manele Bay will give you a vacation experience you won't forget. A luxury resort that overlooks the ocean, you can choose to explore its white sand beaches or indulge in a game of golf in one of its two world-class courses. Elevated above the island's glorious white-sand beach, Four Season's Resort offers an expansive view of the ocean, as well as the spectacular rock formations and red lava cliffs jutting out of the distant coastline.

The over-all theme of the resort is Asian, although there are also slight touches of traditional Hawaiian and Mediterranean styles. Cherry wood, wicker, and rattan are used for the furniture and furnishings, accented by lush and dramatic golden tones. Themed gardens envelop the resort, giving it a relaxing, sophisticated ambience.

You may choose from the 236 guest rooms at the Four Season's Resort Lanai at Manele Bay. For the finest royal treatment, you can pick any of the 21 suites that feature an expansive 34 square meter lanai, a 46-inch LCD television, a king's size bed, and full marble bathroom. For the standard guestrooms, you can expect the best amenities as well, which includes an entertainment center with a 40-inch LCD TV, a private bar, rattan writing desk, and high speed Internet access.

For the guestrooms and suites, you may choose from ocean front rooms or those with an ocean view, a garden view, or a garden-ocean view. The best ocean front rooms offer an open view of the Pacific Ocean, while the ocean view rooms afford a beautiful view of the Hulopoe Bay as well as its bordering coastline. The garden view rooms on the other hand, provides an overlooking view of the resort's well-maintained, lavish gardens. Each of the guestrooms and suites has Hawaiian balconies or lanais, so you can always enjoy the ocean or garden views from your room, while reclining on plush soft-cushioned rattan furniture.

Room rates at the Four Season's Resort Lanai at Manele Bay

Staying at the Four Season's Resort Lanai at Manele Bay can be expensive. However, the services, amenities, and accommodations more than compensate for the high costs. Reservations can be made in advance, and exciting packages for families and honeymooners are also offered. Standard rates typically start at $300+ per night for a guestroom; however the prices can go as high as $7,000 per night if you're taking the most expensive suite. Prices tend to vary during peak and off-peak months however, so it is best to check out the room rates well in advance before booking.

Camping at Hulopoe Beach Park

Hulopoe Beach Park is located in White Manele. According to the locals, Manele Bay is actually divided into two areas, which encompass the White Manele and Black Manele. Hulopoe Beach is located on White Manele, where a magnificent white-gold sand beach awaits sunbathers and swimmers. Since this portion of Manele Bay has a healthy marine life, where species of tropical fish find shelter in beautiful coral reefs and small underwater caves, Hulopoe Beach is also an excellent place for snorkeling.

If you're planning a visit to Manele Bay, but don't want to spend a fortune by staying at its famed luxury resorts, Hulopoe Beach provides the perfect budget accommodation for you. At this beach park, visitors and tourists are allowed to legally camp within designated areas around the beach, after obtaining the right permits from the Lanai

Company. This gives you an unobstructed view of the Manele Bay sunset as well as the star-studded Pacific sky at night. If you have not brought along your own tents, rental tents are available upon request.

Not only is the place inexpensive but, it also offers you access to a beautiful shoreline ideal for swimming and sun bathing. Since the camping permits are good only for a period of seven days, it is best to enjoy the best of Hulopoe Beach during your camping trip. Snorkeling, surfing, and body boarding are just some of the activities you can enjoy here. Coral reef formations, tropical fishes, and magnificent underwater caverns are all waiting to be explored. If you crave for more adventures, you may participate in off shore diving activities, and discover more of the underwater beauty of Manele Bay.

The park has a total of six camp sites, so finding your own private space, whether with friends and family or with loved ones, is easy. You may pitch up tents, gather around a bonfire, or engage in group sports activities. Barbeque sites are available as well, and picnic groves are ideal for intimate or huge gatherings. Restrooms with clean running water and showers are found throughout the camp sites, for a truly comfortable outdoor Hawaiian vacation.

Vacation home rentals at Manele Bay
Those who want to stay at rental accommodations during their vacations at Manele Bay can find a selection of homes, condos, and villas for rent in the area. A rental home is perfect for travelers who want to get reasonably priced accommodations, with all the comforts of home.

Most rental villas are fully furnished, with comfortable living spaces, kitchens, bedrooms, and baths. You can cook your own meals, which means you can save on food expenses while on vacation. If you want to save on your lodging expenses but don't want to camp by the beachside, finding a villa in Manele Bay is the perfect solution for you.

Getting in touch with a rental agent can help you find the Manele Bay rental home that fits your requirements and your budget. Perhaps you might want an oceanfront villa that overlooks the stunning Pacific Ocean. You might require a rental home that can accommodate your friends and family if you're traveling in groups. It is important to find the best possible rental accommodations that suit your unique preferences, for that Hawaiian vacation you will never forget.

Finding the right accommodations at Manele Bay
Manele Bay is frequented by travelers and tourists due to its ideal location, sunny climate, and conveniently located harbour. The white part of

Manele Bay allows you to enjoy world-class golden sand beaches, luxury resorts, camping adventures, as well as a range of water activities from swimming to snorkeling to scuba diving. Black Manele affords you a stunning view of the sea cliffs off the harbour, specifically the Pali Lei no Hauni sea cliffs.

Manele Bay offers a peaceful, relaxing vacation which you can't experience in some of the more populous islands of Hawaii. There are no nightclubs or party venues here. Manele Bay is all about relaxation and comfort, where you can sip a tropical drink watching the sunset on your private lanai, or even as you're gazing at the stars from your camping tent.

Whether you are looking to explore the white part of Manele, or its more dramatic black side, finding the right accommodations for you and your family will help you ensure an unforgettable holiday this side of tropical Hawaii.

Neighborhoods

An Overview of the Neighborhoods and Districts of Lanai

Hawaii is one of the world's most well known and well received vacation destinations. With its grand five-star resorts, shimmering beach coastlines, and mesmerizing natural vistas, it's no wonder why so many people love to come to this group of islands. One of the best islands to visit in Hawaii is Lanai. The small island of Lanai offers a side of Hawaii that few are able to experience when they go to the larger islands, such as Oahu or the Big Island. On Lanai Island, you can experience what island living is all about. The island is hardly inhabited, yet it is packed with some of the best beaches, dramatic island views, and hotel resorts. Although the island is relatively small, it's still a good idea to learn about its neighborhoods and districts. This article will give you some helpful information about the different areas of Lanai Island, so you can navigate around the island easily.

Lanai Island basics

Before going into the specific neighborhoods and districts of Lanai, it's helpful to know where Lanai is among the Hawaiian Islands. Lanai Island is situated right in the middle of Hawaii's main islands. The closest islands to Lanai are Maui to the east and Molokai to the north. Lanai Island is a few miles off the coast of Maui, and many of the people who visit the small island take the ferry from Maui to Lanai for a day-trip. These trips leave the bay of Lahaina in Maui and arrive at Manele Harbor in south Lanai. Aside from the regular ferry, you can also get to Lanai Island by air. Although there are no direct flights from the mainland to Lanai Airport, you can get connecting flights from Honolulu International Airport in Oahu or Kahului Airport in Maui. Lanai Airport is the only airport on the island, and it is located just three miles southwest of Lanai City.

Lanai Island only has a total area of about 140 square miles. This means that the land area of Lanai is roughly the same size as a large city. Raw beauty, however, compensates for what it lacks in size. As you can imagine, such a small area does not have many neighborhoods and districts, but Lanai is conveniently split up into areas, some of which are named after the most popular tourist attractions in the vicinity. "The Secluded Isle," as it is often referred to, is packed with historical sites, incredible beaches, geographic spectacles, and pristine habitats. Whether you want to have a romantic or relaxing Hawaiian vacation, Lanai can be the perfect place for you to visit.

Lanai City
The heart of the island is the small and quiet Lanai City. As the main area on the island where people live, the city is home to a majority of the island's population. Most of the people who live on the island fondly call Lanai City "the village." With the airport so nearby, the village will probably be your first stop when you get off the plane. Although Lanai City is just the size of a village, at about 3.6 square miles in total area, it does have many of the services, amenities, and establishments that you would expect to find in any city. In fact, Lanai City is the main center for the island's commerce and business.

Apart from being the main area of commerce and business, Lanai City is also the island's major cultural and historical center. The city has actually been inducted as one of the most endangered historic sites in the United States. In the 1920s, a man named James Drummond Dole purchased the entire island of Lanai and began to develop the island as a major pineapple plantation. As part of his development efforts, Dole established Lanai City to serve the many workers on the island. The pineapple plantations continued to grow as workers started to come in from other countries such as Japan, the Philippines, China, Korea, and Portugal. The influx of workers from abroad led to the development of the city as a cultural melting pot. Soon, Lanai Island became known as one of the world's largest pineapple plantations, providing a majority of the world's pineapple supply. Once called "Pineapple Isle," a large part of the Lanai Island was converted into pineapple plantations.

During its early years, the city consisted of homes, a jail house, a laundromat, and small shops. Today, however, some of the sites in the city have been torn down in an attempt to make room for tourist attractions, restaurants, hotels, and supermarkets. Lanai City is still home to Dole Park, which is a historic site that stands as a testament to the island's roots as a pineapple plantation. Lanai City is home to Lanai High and Elementary School, which is the only school on the island and the one of the largest K-12 public schools in the education system of Hawaii. You can find some bed and breakfasts in Lanai City, as well as Hotel Lanai, one of the few hotels on the island.

Koele
Just a one-mile drive or hike north of Lanai City is the town of Koele. In the 1860s, a man named Walter Murray Gibson made plans to develop Koele as a Mormon colony for native Hawaiians.

When his plans did not push through, Gibson used the money of the church to purchase parcels of land around the island to be used for ranching. One of these is known today as Koele. The ancient Hawaiian word "Ko'ele" is a name given to a small patch of land that was farmed for the village chief. As Gibson's ranch grew from Koele and around the island, it played an integral role in the growth of the livestock on the island, which included lambs, wild turkeys, horses, cattle, hogs, goats, and sheep.

Today, Koele is home to an award-winning, five-star hotel resort called the Four Seasons Lodge at Koele. You can find an 18-hole, world-class golf range in the area, called The Experience at Koele. Koele is also the starting point for Munro Trail, which snakes up and around the 3,300-foot Mount Lanaihale. From the trail, you can get spectacular views of the Lanai Island and some of the nearby

Hawaiian Islands. Three miles away from Koele are the Luahiwa Petroglyphs, where you can see ancient Hawaiian carvings and stone figures.

Keomuku

Keomuku Village is in the northeastern region of the island. Originally, the area was inhabited by fishing settlements and soon after farming settlements. A boom in the sugar industry led to further development of the Keomuku area. The Maunalei Sugar Company decided to build a railroad track to increase production and speed up distribution. Soon after the track was built, the water mysteriously turned salty and an epidemic wiped out much of the area's population. Legend has it that the company built over sacred stones, disturbing the gods, and leading to the demise of the company and Keomuku's inhabitants. You can visit Keomuku by four-wheel drive vehicle to see Malamalama Church or to visit the six miles of pristine coast line with black sand and clear waters.

South Lanai
South Lanai is another of the island's major areas, where you can find some of the best tourist attractions in Hawaii. First is Hulopoe Beach, on the southern coast of Lanai. This beach has been ranked as one of the best in the country. Manele Bay, which overlooks the beach, is home to one of the award-winning, five-star hotels on the island, the Four Seasons Manele Bay Hotel. May it be diving, snorkeling, swimming, tanning, shopping, or eating, you can find everything you need to relax and have fun at South Lanai.

North Lanai
North Lanai, sometimes referred to as Kanepuu, is northwest of Koele. Although this area is largely uninhabited and doesn't have many tourist facilities, it is full of natural beauty. First is

Kanepu'u Preserve, which is a protected area of dryland forests. Further north is the Garden of the Gods, where you can find lunar-like rock formations that are truly one-of-a-kind. At the north shore is Polihua Beach, where sea turtles nest during the mating season. Just remember that swimming at Polihua Beach is not advised, because of the strong currents. Shipwreck Beach, a historical site that is said to be the wreck site of numerous ships, lies at the end of Keomuku Road.

Visiting Lanai Island
With all of the great places to see and experience on Lanai Island, you definitely won't have a hard time filling up your vacation schedule with activities to participate in and sites to see. Whether you decide to experience the island with the help of a tour guide or you decide to go out and experience it on your own, be sure to pay attention to warning signs about dangerous

beaches or trails. A map will also help you navigate through the island and explore different points of interest. Also, remember to bring your camera along, because you will definitely want to have pictures of this unbelievably beautiful island.

Sporting Activities in Lanai

Lanai, with all its beautiful sceneries and its many interesting geological features, is a must-see for any tourist. Its pristine beaches and clear blue water have attracted and continue to attract many vacationers. The island's rainforests are also a sight to behold. If you think, these are enough reasons to visit Lanai, wait until you see the island's offerings of amazing geological wonders. Located south of Lanai City is the Puu Pehe or the Sweetheart Rock. This 80-foot rock is considered one of the most celebrated landmarks on the island and it never fails to amaze the tourists who visit the area. Another magnificent geological wonder that you will see on the island is the Garden of the Gods. Contrary to its name, the site is not a place where you will find blooming flowers. Instead, what you will see there are rocks and boulders of varying colors, sizes and shapes. Why the name then? According to legends, the boulders and rocks found in the area actually fell from the garden of the gods in the sky while the gods tended their garden.

There is no doubt that Lanai is an ideal place for sightseeing and relaxation but you will be surprised to know that the island is also an excellent venue for many fun outdoor activities. Its varied terrain and other physical features make Lanai one of the best places to engage in sports ranging from the most ordinary to those that border on the extreme. Below are just some of these activities that you can enjoy while on the island of Lanai.

Golf

If you are one of the many who live to play golf, you will find Lanai to be a paradise. Depending on your preference, your level of expertise and your budget, you can find a golf course that is just right for you. The island has a very popular golf course, The Challenge. This three-hole golf course at Manele designed by Jack Nicklaus is built on lava outcroppings. Another excellent thing about this golf course is that every hole provides an excellent view of the Pacific ocean. You will also find the golf course complete with necessary facilities such as rental clubs, driving range, putting green, bar, restaurant, and pro-shop. If you are not into this sport yet, The Challenge is also a great place to learn it. You can take lessons there and be on your way to becoming a pro in no time.

Not as well known as The Challenge but beginning to become popular is a golf course in Koele known as The Experience. The course was designed by Greg Norman. This golf course is famous for its incredible terrain, its elevation, range of play challenges, and the architecture of the landscape. The Experience also offers lessons, and driving range, putting green, rental clubs, restaurant, bar, and pro-shop can also be found there. If you are on a budget, you can still play golf in the nine-holer Cavendish Golf Course. You don't have to pay a specific amount for this course, a donation will do. This course was designed by E.B Cavendish during the heyday of the pineapple plantation. This golf course, however, cannot be compared with either the Challenge or The Experience in that it has no starter, no clubhouse, and no phone.

Tennis

A game of tennis would also not be far from the list of what to do in Lanai especially if you book your accommodations at either Manele Bay Hotel or the Lodge at koele. This is because from there, you have easy access to the Tennis Center at Manele. The center has six plexipave courts and offers facilities such as the tournament facilities and the pro shop. You will also find a number of tennis courts at Koele. Aside from those courts, you can also make use of public tennis courts for free but you have to make sure you have made reservations before you go there to play.

Biking
What about mixing sightseeing with getting your daily dose of exercise? Biking is the sport for you then. Lanai offers excellent trails for bikers. From the city, you can follow the route going north. You then have to make your way through the former pineapple fields and the magnificent Garden of the

Gods. With the beautiful sceneries that await the bikers, biking is an activity that you should not miss doing while in Lanai. Unfortunately, not everybody can go biking hassle-free because there are not that many bike rentals in the area and usually, only guests of resorts with bike rental facilities can engage in this activity.

Hiking
One of the favorite activities of those who go to Lanai is hiking. With the beautiful sceneries you will see along the way, you will not feel tired. The hiking trails in the island will take you to secluded beaches, forests, and incredible sites such as the Garden of the Gods. One of the popular trails is the Lanai Fisherman Trail. So called because the fisherman in the area use this trail to go to their fishing spot. Another well-known hiking trail is the Koloiki Ridge. This trail starts behind the Lodge at Koele. Along the way, you will see the Views of

Maui, Molokai, Naio Gulch, and Maunalei Valley. The Munro Trail is also a popular one and is considered one of the most challenging trails.

Camping

If you want to enjoy outdoor activity, nothing beats camping. It would be an excellent experience if you could stay outside for a whole day drinking in the beauty of nature. Just imagine yourself enjoying the freshness of the air outdoor, sitting on the grassy camping ground, or watching the star-studded sky while you lie on your back. Doing these things would really make your vacation a memorable and fun-filled one. This is why, you should not miss camping when you visit the island. You can opt to camp at Castle and Cooke Resorts Campground. Hulopoe Beach also offers a grassy camping ground. There are various camping facilities in this site. These include barbecue grills, beach side showers, in case you want to dip in the water nearby, and clean restrooms. Cutting firewood is prohibited in this place, so you have to buy charcoal in the city before you head off to this site.

Deep-Sea Fishing
Being an island, Lanai is not just a haven for those who love to engage in land-based activities. It is even a more fantastic place for those who enjoy water sports. One water activity that you can enjoy in the waters of Lanai is deep-sea fishing. For deep-sea fishing, the ferry departs from Manele Harbor very early in the morning, around six o'clock. You can enjoy good catches all year round. But it is in summer and spring that the catches are really excellent. Among the fishes you can have the chance to catch are the prized Mahimahi, ono, marlin, and ahi.

Swimming

Hawaii is famous for its beaches so your Hawaiian vacation would not be complete without plunging into its crystal blue waters. There are various excellent beaches in Lanai. One of these is the Hulopoe Beach. You can find a lot of palm trees on this beach and the sand is of golden hue. The colorful fishes that you will see underwater are simply magnificent. It's no wonder this beach was ranked by Dr. Stephen Leatherman, a professional beach surveyor, as the best beach in the US in 1997. You can also opt to go to Polihua Beach. However, you have to be careful swimming in this beach because of the strong current.

Scuba Diving
The water of Lanai is home to various species of colorful fishes. The place also has many acclaimed cavern dive sites that make the waters of the island a scuba diver's paradise. The dive site Cathedral, near Hulopoe Bay, is considered the

best cavern dive site in the Pacific by Skin Diver magazine. This cavern is composed of lava ridges, an archway, and a cave.

Kayaking
Kayaking is another fun activity you can do while on the island. Manta rays and sea turtles can be your company while you kayak in the blue water. The view of the long stretches of coast line is also one of the things that make kayaking enjoyable. If you want to go kayaking, it is necessary that you know how to swim. It is also advisable that you do kayaking in the early morning because the water is calmer at such time. It is important that you transact with a kayak owner from Maui beforehand because there are no rentals in Lanai.

Surfing
Another water sport you can enjoy in Lanai is surfing. For beginners, the southeast-facing breaks at Lopa Beach is an excellent spot. If you want a

more challenging surfing spot, you should try the waters of Hulopoe Bay. If you don't know how to surf, you should not miss taking surfing lessons here.

Snorkeling
Snorkeling is one of the easiest sports you can enjoy in Lanai. It is also one of the most enjoyable. With the richness of the underwater life in lanai, you would surely find this sport really fun. You can bring your own snorkeling equipment, rent one from your hotel, or buy it in Lanai city.

The island of Lanai is not just a place that holds a feast for the eyes, it is also definitely a sportsman's paradise.

The Cuisine of Lanai

Lanai is one of smallest islands of Hawaii. But even though it is less developed than the other islands, it has much to offer to visiting tourists. Lanai does possess a certain charm that makes it the island of choice of many city dwellers and adventure travelers. Bill Gates, for one, chose Lanai to be the venue of his wedding in 1994. Perhaps the world-famous billionaire found the privacy and serenity he wanted for celebrating a special day in his life. The same is true for people from around the world who come to visit Lanai all-year round to spend vacation, take part in festivals, and hold their weddings. It's not called the "The Secluded Island" for no reason at all.

Here in Lanai, you won't find any traffic light or endless stretch of paved road. Instead, you'll be surrounded by lush greenery and sandy beaches, which serve as a good backdrop for oceanfront dining that's popular in the island. Aside from the friendliness of the people, the spectacular view of the ocean and mountain peaks, dining here in Lanai is something to look forward to. With its wide array of dishes and mix of culinary influences, it is in Lanai where you'll get a true taste of Pacific Rim flavors.

Hawaiian dining

You'd probably think that because of the rich soils of Hawaii, it was fairly easy for them to infuse new flavors to their dishes using the local ingredients. But the gustatory delights Hawaii is known for were not made overnight. There was even a time when locals mostly enjoyed packed food that came from the US. Popular treats back then were frozen pizza and its world-famous pineapple. But as time went by and as tourists soon flock to the islands of Hawaii, local dining only became more exciting. Different ingredients were grown to add new and fresh flavors to their homegrown recipes. The plantation days also brought in different culinary recipes from the Philippines, Korea, Japan, and even Portugal.

It is here in Hawaii where you'll find a good mix of traditional oriental cooking and dishes from the Western world. From these, they infused their own styles of cooking and tried to diversify by adding new flavors that are native to the island. These specialties are commonly served in the famous luaus and Hawaiian festivals. There are also local diners and beachfront restaurants that offer a wide array of Hawaiian dishes in their menu. Today, Hawaii is not just known for its sweet pineapples but also for its Pacific Rim flavors that were cultivated over the years.

Dishes in Lanai

Here in Lanai, poi remains to be a staple food, commonly served in luaus and even as ordinary home meal. It is a sticky purple paste made from the taro plant. Poi actually plays a big role in their culture. It is said that with poi on the table, people around it should not engage in any fight or argument. This is because poi is a symbol used to represent the ancestor of chiefs and the native Hawaiians.

The people of Lanai also carry the tradition of roasting pig during special occasions. The inhabitants of this island also takes advantage of the rich marine life. Many of their cuisines are actually prepared using seafood. Locals take pride in their seafood specialties. These dishes are sprinkled with just the right herbs, spices, and other ingredients to add flavor to fresh catches.

The native Hawaiian dishes are just part of the island's cuisine. Like everything else in Lanai, many cuisines have been influenced by diverse cultures. In this island, you can actually sample various types of dishes, from native Hawaiian, European, and Japanese to the fusion of all these.

If you're in for a week-long vacation in Lanai, you'll have all the time you need to dine in all its restaurants. There are just a little over 10 restaurants here. While some of the dining estalibshments are downright luxurious, some are just right even for a tight budget. In any of these restaurants, you'll surely receive the gift of the "aloha" spirit from its service crew.

Fist-class restaurants in Lanai

The two major resorts in the island can offer you a fine dining experience. Lodge at Koele's Formal Dining Room and Manele Bay Hotel's Ihilani Restaurant are both listed in Gourmet Magazine as among the best restaurants in Hawaii. Lodge at Koele's Fomarl Dining Room serves mostly American cuisines, while the Ihilani Restaurant of Manele Bay Hotel offers French cuisine. Here in Ihilani, you have the poached lobster, foie gras, and Porcini mushroom soup as among your menu choices. Both Ihilani and The Lodge at Koele require formal wear.

Henry Clay's Rotisserie in Hotel Lanai is also one of the best restaurants in the island that serve American cuisine. Among the culinary specialties of this establishment are seafood dishes and rotisserie meats. Henry Clay's Rotisserie is also acclaimed for its pecan pie. Compared to the above-mentioned restaurants, Henry Clay's Rotisserie has a more laid-back ambiance.

The Terrace Restaurant of Lodge at Koele offers American cuisine as well. The menu includes burger, salads, and sandwiches. while dining in this place, you can watch the beautiful garden and pine forests through its glass walls.

The Challenge at Manele Clubhouse is best known for its fish tacos, ahi sashimi, and Chinese barbecued chicken salad. This restaurant provides a nice view of the Pacific Ocean. If you want to try a combination of various cuisines, you should visit Hulopoe Court, which is found in the Four Seasons Resort at Manele Bay. This restaurant has received accolades for its Pacific Rim seafood dishes. Aside from serving sumptuous cuisines, it also offers excellent oceanview from every table.

Restaurants with laid-back atmosphere

Pele's Other Garden is another recommended dining place in Lanai. It offers gourmet deli, from sandwiches and pizzas to many more delectable snacks. Pele's Other Garden can provide you with a picnic basket if you want to tour around the place. The best thing about this dining place is that it transforms into an Italian Bistro by night.

If you want a poolside dining experience, Ocean Grille is an ideal choice for you. Here, you can dine during or after you dip in the water. This tropical bar provides drinks and smoothies, salads, burgers, and sandwiches, among other island specials. This establishment is popular for its basket of taro chips.

You can also enjoy a more laid-back ambiance in Blue Ginger Cafe. Its menu includes spam, egg, burgers, sandwiches, and Portuguese sausages. You can also opt to have your juicy burgers from Tanigawa's. Here, you'll surely enjoy meat dishes. If you want to sample a blend of Lanai's ethnic and local cuisines you can go to Cafe 565, which serves pizza, salads, and sandwiches. If you are fond of ice creams, you should not miss the Sweetest Days Ice Cream, where you can buy scoops of your favorite ice cream flavor and other desserts.

If you want to experience the famous luau or the traditional party of the Hawaiians, you can make arrangements with the Four Seasons Resort Lanai at Manele Bay.

Most of the restaurants in Lanai do not have delivery services, so you really have to go to the restaurants to have your meal. It would be worth it because the dishes are not the only things to look forward to, you'll also enjoy the view, the ambiance, and service from the friendly staff who are always ready with their smiles. Many of the establishments are located in beach front, where you will surely have a view of the clear waters, powdery sands, and tropical trees.

Remember to make reservations in fine dining restaurants to get a good seat and ensure accommodation. In restaurants for middle-class budget, there is no need for you to dress up formally. You can just wear anything comfortable.

Food booths

During festivals, there are also cooking contests where you will see how people prepare different cuisines. Aside from this, there are lots of booths that sell food and beverages. If you attend the Pineapple Festival, for instance, you can sample the different dishes from these booths. During Lanai's Aloha Festival, you will also find food stations that serve Hawaiian favorites. What's great about this experience is that you will get the chance to mingle with the locals and tourists alike. This is a good opportunity for you to hear their stories and travel experiences.

Your dining experience in Lanai won't be complete if you miss the island's local cuisine. You have to include in your itinerary restaurants that serve local favorites. Budget don't have to be much of a problem. There are lots of restaurants in this island that offer excellent Lanaian cuisines without burning a hole in your pocket.

Other than good-tasting food, there are a lot of things to make your dining experience in Lanai memorable. The magnificent view of the beach and the lush greenery in the island would also whet your appetite. Another essential part of the Lanaian dining experience is the warm welcome and the hospitality of the people.

What to do in Lanai

Once known as "The Pineapple Isle, the island of Lanai in Hawaii is often referred to today as "The Secluded Isle." Although it is one of the smallest inhabited islands in Hawaii, it is packed with some of the greatest and most unique activities in all of the Hawaiian Islands. Whether you are planning to go to Hawaii for your honeymoon and wedding or summer vacation and family trip, there are tons of things that you can do on this pint-sized island. From visits to historical sites to adventurous off-road trips, you can plan the perfect Hawaii getaway on Lanai Island. Read on to learn more about some of the attractions and things to do while on Lanai.

Lanai City

Whenever it's your first trip to a vacation destination, there are always some locations that you can't miss out on. Although Lanai is small, it has some sites that you just have to see. First on the list is Lanai City. Fondly referred to as "the village," Lanai City is a small, friendly, and welcoming place where there are no stop lights or traffic jams. It's also one of the few places on the island with paved roads. Lanai City is right at the heart of the island, where the elevation is about 1,700 feet up the side of Mount Lanaihale. Two hotels in Lanai City are the five-star Lodge at Koele and the historic Hotel Lanai. You may also want to stay at one of the bed and breakfasts in the city, so you can really get a feel of what daily life is like on the island. Most of the shops, vehicle rentals, and other tourist services are located in Lanai City.

Munro Trail and Mount Lanaihale
Just ten minutes north of Lanai City is one of the famous wonders of Lanai that you definitely have to experience: Munro Trail. Although experienced hikers can tackle Munro Trail in about half or three-fourths of a day, it would be wise to hire a tour guide who can tell you all about the breathtaking landscapes, historic sites, and amazing island culture. Named after a New Zealand naturalist named George Munro, this trail offers one of the most convenient, amazing, and adventurous ways to experience the whole of Lanai Island. Just under ten miles long, Munro Trail starts north of Lanai City, about 100 feet above the city.

Along your hike or four-wheel adventure on Munro Trail, you will wind around the island seeing some of the best views that Hawaii has to offer. Part of the trail is the uphill trek to the highest point of Lanai Island, which is the peak of Mount Lanaihale at about 3,370 feet above sea level. From this summit, you can see other Hawaiian main islands, including Oahu, Molokai, Maui, and The Big Island. You'll also get to see the white sand beaches, the fresh pine trees, the canyons of Maunalei gulch. Whether you decide to take a tour guide or not, make sure you come prepared for Munro Trail, because it does have some challenging areas. Grab your jackets, your cameras, some drinks and food for a great trip along Munro Trail.

The Garden of the Gods
When you first hear the name "Garden of the Gods," you may think of a colorful garden

abounding with flowers and plant life, but Lanai's Keahiakawelo or Garden of the Gods is something you will just have to see to believe. If you've ever wanted to walk upon the rugged landscapes of the moon, Lanai's Keahiakawelo might just be the perfect place for you to go. With its unbelievable rock formations, Keahiakawelo is another worldly garden where you can get a glimpse of nature's creativity and beauty.

One of the great benefits of going to the Garden of the Gods is that you can get in touch with the legendary lore that is so ingrained in Hawaiian culture. According to ancient Hawaiian beliefs, the Garden of the Gods was created when two priests, called "kahuna," competed to have the longest-burning fire. In an attempt to win the contest against the kahuna of Molokai, the kahuna of Lanai used all of the vegetation around the Keahiakawelo area, leaving nothing behind but dust and rocks. Today, you can visit the Garden of the Gods to see amazing rock formations, including towers, crater-like surfaces, and bizarre rock gardens. Perhaps the best way to tour the Garden of the Gods is to rent some four-by-four vehicles so you can rough it out on your rock garden adventure. You definitely won't be seeing formations like this again, so you might want to bring your camera along. Although many people love the beach sunsets of Hawaii, watching the sun set at the Garden of the Gods can be just as exciting, with brilliant colors bouncing off the rocks.

Hulopoe Bay
Not only has Hulopoe Bay been voted as one of the top ten beaches in Hawaii, but it is also ranked as one of the top beaches in the country. Just at the south coast of Lanai, Hulopoe Bay is a favorite spot for tourists who want to relax and enjoy one of the

best tourist attractions that Hawaii has to offer: the beach. Overlooking Hulopoe Beach is the Four Seasons Resort and Spa at Manele Bay, one of Lanai's five-star resorts. Whether or not you are staying at the Four Seasons Resort and Spa, visiting Hulopoe Beach should still be on your list when you travel to Lanai.

If you come to Hulopoe Beach during the summer, then you should definitely take advantage of the relatively calm tides and take a dip in the deep blue waters. You can snorkel to view the colorful sea life, you can sunbathe to enjoy the beautiful scenery, or you can have a nice picnic along the beach and just soak it all in. Another great activity while you're down at Hulopoe Beach is dolphin and whale watching. Just remember that Manele Bay and Hulopoe Bay are both part of the Manele-Hulopoe Marine Sanctuary. This means that the locals and the officials all try to do their part in preserving the natural beauty of the bays. They also ask visitors to help take care of the beaches by avoiding taking home shells, wildlife, and plants.

Although summer is the ideal place to visit Hulopoe Bay, there are still loads of activities for those who come during the winter. Even if the seas are a bit choppy and the tides get strong around winter time, you can enjoy the other side of Hulopoe Bay: the resort. The Four Seasons Resort and Spa is an award-winning hotel resort where you can find shops, restaurants, and many other amenities that you would expect to find in a five-star resort. As if fine dining and shopping weren't enough, you can also get full treatments at the spa. Whatever it is you decide to do, make sure you have a great time at this one-of-a-kind beach.

The Challenge at Manele
Aptly named, The Challenge at Manele is a golf course that gives even some of the best golfers an

exciting feat. What's unique about this golf course is that nature has played a big role in forming some of its most challenging areas. From lava-formed obstructions to dipping cliffs that run straight down into the Pacific, you are not only given the challenge of taking on this five-tee course, but you will also get some of the best views of the island. Just make sure that you don't get too distracted by the whales that you can see from the course.

The Experience at Koele
For those who want a more immersive golfing experience, then The Experience at Koele may just be the perfect choice. This 18-hole course is at an elevation of about 2,000 feet, offering some nice views of the island, aside from the beauty of the course itself. Pine trees, ravines, channels, streams, lakes, and waterfalls are just some of the

sites that you can see from this course, which was designed by Ted Robinson and Greg Norman.

Other attractions and things to do in Lanai

Lanai is definitely one of the most unique and untouched islands in Hawaii. You might think that this small island doesn't have all of the frills and thrills of some of the bigger, more inhabited, and better developed Hawaiian Islands. In truth, however, Lanai can offer many of the amenities, attractions, and activities in other Hawaiian Islands and more. From horseback riding and hiking to snorkeling and off-road adventuring, you can be sure that you'll be able to fill up your Lanai travel itinerary. Here are some of the other places that you may want to visit while on Lanai Island:

Kaunolu - Kaunolu is a historical site that was once the favorite fishing spot of King Kamehameha I, the first king of the Kingdom of Hawaii.

Dole Park - Dole Park is a historical site that was established by the Dole Food Company when they owned the island and turned it into the world's largest pineapple producer.

Palawai Basin - This is the site of Lanai's well known pineapple plantations. Considering how small Lanai is, it's hard to believe that this island once produced majority of the world's pineapple supply.

Luahiwa Petroglyphs - These are rock etchings and sculptures that were made by ancient Hawaiians when they first arrived on the island in the 1500's.

Kanepuu Preserve - This is around 590 acres of protected forest with over 40 native plant species.

Shipwreck Beach - This historical landmark features eight miles of beach where numerous ships have ended in a wreck because of the rocky and shallow waters.

Getting to Lanai

Lanai is considered as one of the Hawaiian islands that are not yet tainted with modernity. Although Lanai offers conveniences that would ensure your comfort while you stay there, it is not cramped with skyscrapers, traffic jams, traffic lights, and large shopping centers that are commonly found in many cities. This island has beauty which only nature can provide--long stretches of sandy beaches, sparkling waters of the Pacific, tree-lined streets, houses graced with blooming gardens, and refreshing vast grasslands that were once pineapple plantations.

Lanai has first class hotels and resorts that would not just make your stay in the island comfortable, but also fun. The Four Seasons Resort, for instance, can make your stay enjoyable through the facilities it provides such as spas and its golf course. The place also has lots of award-winning restaurants where you can have a variety of options when dining out, from American, European, to native Hawaiian dishes.

You can also opt to explore the city center where you can feast your eyes on the historic buildings of the island, which dates back to the early 1920s when Lanai city was still a pineapple plantation town. This historic site is now threatened by commercial developement. To preserve this historic treasure, Lanai City was declared as one of the most endangered historic areas in the country.

Aside from sightseeing, you can do a lot of fun activities in Lanai such as swimming, boating, kayaking, snorkeling, and hiking. This island is also home to the popular golf-course at the Manele Bay Resort, popularly known as "The Challenge." So if you are fond of playing golf, you just need to go to the Four Seasons Resort in Manele Bay.

How to go to Lanai
To reach the exciting island of Lanai, you have various options. If you are from the mainland or from any other country, you have to fly first to Honolulu International Airport. Then, you should look for local airlines that fly to Lanai Airport. Some of these Hawaiiaan airlines that service tourists are the Island Air and the Hawaiian Airlines. Jet planes also fly to this island, but provide less frequent services for tourists compared to local airlines.

Tips and Tricks for the Traveler

Hawaii is a place where you can experience things that you won't be able to experience anywhere else. The culture and tradition of the people of Hawaii is so rich that that alone can make your vacation memorable. Here, the past intermingles with the present, and rustic simplicity merges with modern sophistication, creating a uniquely Hawaiian experience. Hawaii is known for its many beautiful islands and the best thing about that is that each of these islands has something unique to offer to tourists.

One of the islands that has much to offer is Lanai. Used to be known as the Pineapple Island because it was once home to one of the world's largest pineapple plantations, today, Lanai is known more as The Secluded Island. This is not because it is remote or uninhabited but because despite the number of tourists flocking here all year round, the island maintains its rusticity. Among the islands of Hawaii, it is one of those that give the impression of a paradise yet to be explored and discovered. Elements of metropolitan sophistication is not commonly found here, except at the Four Seasons

Resort. The said resort stands like a palace amidst the almost surreal beauty of the surroundings. The azure sea, the golden beach sand, the verdant forests and grasslands, and the wine colored sunset sky are among the things that make Lanai a place that is worth visiting.

Although a vacation to this island of Hawaii may be a bit costly, there are ways to make your vacation in this paradise enjoyable without bleeding your savings dry. Below are some tips and tricks that could help you maximise your fun while you are on the island.

Places you should not miss while on Lanai
There are so many things to see and do in Lanai. To make sure that you get to see the most interesting places and truly experience Lanai, you should know what the most popular sites here are. One of the places that the people of Lanai are so proud of is the Garden of the Gods.There you will find

impressive rocks and boulders standing on a vast desert-like stretch of land. These boulders look like plants proudly standing on a vast garden. Another landmark you should not miss is the Sweetheart Rock, which is located off shore. This is a majestic rock, which some locals believe to be haunted by the spirit of a maiden who was buried there by her lover. The legend about this place, which is romantic and at the same time a bit creepy, is just one of the many interesting stories you will hear from the locals that explain the existence and appearance of some of the island's landmarks.

The beaches are also not to be missed. If you go to the famous Shipwreck Beach, you will surely be amazed by the remnant of a ship from the 1940s. If you look at it from the shore, you will find the shipwreck surreal, especially during foggy days. If you are one for the bizarre, you will most enjoy this view at dusk, especially when the dying sun casts its wine-colored light on the background making the shipwreck look eerie.

How to go to Lanai
There are two major means by which to reach Lanai. One is through a plane and the other is through a ferry. If you are going to take a plane, you still have to fly first to Honolulu and then take a plane to Lanai. The airport in this island is a 10-minute drive from the city center. If you are staying at the Four Seasons Resort or at the Hotel Lanai, you can take the shuttle. If you are going to take the ferry, you should know that it makes seven trips a day from Maui. The ferry will take you to Manele Bay Harbor within 75 minutes if you are coming from Ma'alaea, Maui. It would take 45 minutes if you are going to Lanai from Lahaina, Maui. Although a ferry ride can be tough during winter, it is the best time to see some spinner dolphins on the way. If you are staying at the Four

Seasons resort, you can take a shuttle from the port to the resort. But if you are not going to stay at the said resort, you can just take a bus or hire a van. For a more convenient way to explore Lanai, you can rent a car. In this way, you can go and stop anywhere and anytime you want.

Where to stay
If you want to enjoy a luxurious stay in Lanai and you have the money to splurge on luxurious accommodations, you can make reservations at the Lodge at Koele or at Manele Bay Hotel. The English-style accommodations will really give you the best comforts while you are on the island. Aside from that, you can also access some of the island's best restaurants and golf facilities if you stay there. If you don't have that much money to spend, you can still find comfortable accommodations for a lesser rate at the Lanai Hotel. If you are on a budget, there are lots of Bed

and Breakfasts where you can find accommodations for even less. If you are bringing along your family, house rentals is a good choice to save on money.

Restaurants in Lanai
There are various restaurants in Lanai. You can go and dine at the luxurious restaurants in Manele Bay Hotel or at the Lodge in Koele. Here, American and European cuisines are the specialty. Aside from the exquisite-tasting food, you will also find that the excellent view in those restaurants adds to the unforgetableness of your dining experience there. However, again expect that such an experience comes with a price so if you are not one to splurge on food or the ambiance, there are many other less costly restaurants and bars you can check out. Usually the dishes served in those restaurants are combinations of different cuisines, from native Hawaiian to Japanese to American and

European cuisines. The best thing about these smaller restaurants and bars is that they can provide you a taste of truly Lanaian cuisine.

Activities you can do in Lanai
Lanai is not only a place where you can relax. This island is also a place where you can enjoy various activities. One of these is biking. The red-dirt roads on the island are excellent biking trails. Along the way, you will get the chance to see beautiful and wonderful sceneries. Aside from this, you can also play golf. The Manele Bay Hotel and the Lodge offer two famous golf courses, the Experience at Koele and the Challenge at Manele. These courses have facilities that would make your golfing experience fun. If you prefer water activities, Lanai is also known for its beautiful waters. Here you can do swimming, kayaking, snorkeling, and scuba diving. The Hulopoe Beach is one of the best beaches to visit while in Lanai. Aside from the

inviting blue water, you will also find excellent panorama there. The place is also rich in marine life, making it ideal for scuba diving and snorkeling. You can also treat yourself to a view of the magnificent whales in Polihua Beach. If you visit Lanai in the winter months, you will see a lot of these sea creatures. Camping is also enjoyable here. You can stay outdoor through the night just gazing at the stars. You should not also miss hiking during your vacation. There are many hiking trails in Lanai. Hiking will enable you to see many of the island's landmarks. Another thrilling and popular activity is cliff diving. It is said that this sport was started by the Hawaiian King Kahekili. According to accounts, he commanded his followers to jump off the cliff in order to prove their loyalty and courage. Later, the famous King Kamehameha made this practice a competition.

How to find an excellent travel deal to Lanai

One of the best ways to find an excellent vacation package to Hawaii is by planning several months before your desired vacation schedule. In this way, you will have enough time to search for the deal that would not make a hole in your pocket. You will also find less expensive vacation packages if you schedule your vacation during the off season. Because there aren't that many visitors during this season, hotels and airlines usually lower their rates. It is also important to make your reservations in advance because the rates may quickly change.

What you should bring to Lanai
If you are an American citizen, you are not required to present your passport. Otherwise, you should present one. You need to bring valid IDs as you may need them for renting cars or doing other transactions. Although there are shops where you can purchase the things you need, it is better to

bring stuff such as your sunblock and sunglasses for these may come expensive if you are going to purchase them from the shops in Lanai. Unless you are planning to dine in the luxurious resorts in the island or planning to attend a formal event such as a wedding, you don't have to bring formal wear. You can just bring clothes that you are most comfortable wearing. You may also bring sweater for the cool nights.

The End

www.ingramcontent.com/pod-product-compliance
Lightning Source LLC
Chambersburg PA
CBHW031110080526
44587CB00011B/905